T0353707

The
EMOTIONAL CYCLE
of DEPLOYMENT

Understanding the Emotional Cycle and
Its Impact on Military Families

ALLISON BRATTON, MS, LPC

BALBOA.PRESS
A DIVISION OF HAY HOUSE

Balboa Press books may be ordered through booksellers or by contacting:

Balboa Press
A Division of Hay House
1663 Liberty Drive
Bloomington, IN 47403
www.balboapress.com
844-682-1282

Because of the dynamic nature of the Internet, any web addresses or links contained in this book may have changed since publication and may no longer be valid. The views expressed in this work are solely those of the author and do not necessarily reflect the views of the publisher, and the publisher hereby disclaims any responsibility for them.

The author of this book does not dispense medical advice or prescribe the use of any technique as a form of treatment for physical, emotional, or medical problems without the advice of a physician, either directly or indirectly. The intent of the author is only to offer information of a general nature to help you in your quest for emotional and spiritual well-being. In the event you use any of the information in this book for yourself, which is your constitutional right, the author and the publisher assume no responsibility for your actions.

Any people depicted in stock imagery provided by Getty Images are models, and such images are being used for illustrative purposes only. Certain stock imagery © Getty Images.

Print information available on the last page.

ISBN: 979-8-7652-5338-0 (sc)
ISBN: 979-8-7652-5339-7 (hc)
ISBN: 979-8-7652-5337-3 (e)

Library of Congress Control Number: 2024912612

Balboa Press rev. date: 09/30/2024

DEDICATION

This book is dedicated to all the military families who refuse to be statistics and to all of the families who are determined to build resiliency, understand each other, and love one another unconditionally.

The one constant in life is change. Change is hard. Change is uncomfortable. Change shakes our sense of safety and security, but without it, growth would not be possible.

People generally do well with predictability and consistency. These qualities are valued throughout society and are challenging to maintain in every aspect of life. The world changes every day. My world changes every day, and change is needed to help us become the absolute best versions of ourselves that we can be.

The only constant is change. That means we spend a lot of time and energy coping with that change and spend time and energy trying to incorporate consistency and predictability into this new change. Most people learn from resisting the change and making destructive decisions that bring momentary comfort.

My goal is to ease that discomfort a little bit. Luckily, we have the option to choose the destructive way we reacted to change in the past or decide we need to pivot and make another choice.

We can make different choices. We can choose again and again and again. Hopefully, when we choose again, we have gained the knowledge to make healthier choices by mindfully choosing again.

ABOUT THE AUTHOR
Allison Bratton LPC

Allison *won* a first publishing master's package from Balboa Publishing after submitting a book proposal for this book to a Hay House Publishing contest in 2023.

Allison's experiences as a military spouse and professional counselor have given her valuable insights into the unique challenges that military families face. She is passionate about providing support and guidance to those who serve our country and their loved ones.

Allison earned her bachelor's degree in business administration and organizational development from American InterContinental University while being stationed at Naval Air Station Sigonella, Italy.

In 2007, they were transferred to Virginia Beach (Naval Air Station Oceana) where they continued to build their life together as a family. While Allison's husband Derek was deployed, she moved back to her mother's and worked as a preschool teacher and volunteer at the Shelter from the Storm women's domestic violence shelter.

In 2011, their family was stationed as NAS Fallon, Nevada. Allison worked at the Navy Gate Way Inn and Suites as a receptionist and at the Western Nevada Regional Youth Center as a counselor.

In 2017, Allison was awarded a master's degree in marriage and family therapy and professional Christian counseling from Grand Canyon University with honors. Allison started her master's degree while living in Nevada and finished it while living in California.

She held an associate marriage and family therapy license in California and moved to Oregon in 2018.

In 2021, she became a licensed practicing counselor with the state of Oregon.

Allison faced challenges of balancing her career aspirations with the demands of military life, frequent moves, and deployments.

Allison had to quickly adapt to new environments and immerse herself in diverse cultures.

Despite these challenges, she approached each location with a positive attitude and dedicated herself to helping those in need. This included working with individuals struggling with drugs, alcohol, domestic violence, as well as children, adolescents, and military families.

Allison's dedication and determination have not gone unnoticed. She was awarded her degree while her two older children sat with her coworkers at the ceremony held at the base chapel. Her youngest child Felicity, who was one year old, was in the base daycare at the time, and Allison's husband Derek was deployed.

Through her own experiences as a military spouse and professional counselor, Allison has gained valuable insights into the unique challenges that military families face. She is passionate about providing support and guidance to those who serve our country and their loved ones.

Being a military spouse is no easy feat. It requires immense strength, resilience, and adaptability. Every day comes with its own set of challenges, be it dealing with deployments, moving to new locations, or managing the household alone while your partner is away on duty.

Allison knows this all too well. She is married to her husband Derek, who is now retired from the military after twenty years of service. Allison had to navigate through numerous obstacles and responsibilities that come with being a military spouse. These included taking care of their home and children while he was deployed, supporting him emotionally from afar, and tirelessly working to improve the future of her family, her clients, and the military spouse community as a whole.

Allison's career began when she was in California volunteering with a women's domestic violence shelter while Derek was deployed. She worked on base with the Fleet and Family Service Center in 2015. The Fleet and Family Service Center is a one-stop shop for all active duty, retired, and gold-star military families. They provide a wide variety of services from clinical counseling, new parent support services, child and youth programs, relocation assistance, resume workshops and employment assistance, return and reunion support, classes, and groups. The list is extensive. In 2018, Allison began working as a behavior health specialist at the prestigious Oregon State Hospital. This position allowed her to gain valuable experience and knowledge while also providing care for individuals with severe mental illness.

In addition to her work at the hospital, Allison has her own counseling practice located in downtown Silverton, Oregon. She helps Oregonians of all ages and backgrounds improve their mental health and overall well-being. She also has an online coaching business where she can continue to provide support for active-duty spouses experiencing deployment.

Whether it's helping couples strengthen their relationships or working with individuals dealing with mental health issues, Allison is committed to making a positive impact in the lives of others. With her extensive knowledge and compassionate approach, she continues to make a difference in the military community and beyond.

Allison's story serves as an inspiration to many and showcases the resilience and dedication of military spouses. Her journey also highlights the vital role that mental health professionals play in supporting and strengthening military families. As a result, Allison's work is not only meaningful but essential in creating a better future for those who serve our country.

Her dedication and hard work are a true testament to the values of service and sacrifice that are at the core of the military lifestyle. Her story is a reminder of the strength and resilience that exists within military communities.

Allison's book is a compilation of her personal experiences and the work she has done with the emotional cycle of deployment. Her goal is to raise awareness and help others understand this crucial aspect of military life. By understanding the cycle, families can better navigate through the challenges of deployment and maintain healthy relationships.

Allison wants to share her story not just for herself, but for the countless other spouses out there who may be struggling to navigate this lifestyle. Her hope is that her journey can bring a sense of understanding, comfort, and support to others in similar situations.

Disclaimer: While every effort has been made to offer accurate advice, the content is meant to provide general guidance. Individual circumstances may require tailored approaches from healthcare or mental health professionals. The author has made every effort to ensure that the information in this book was correct at press time. The author does not assume and hereby disclaims any liability to any party for any loss, damage, or disruption caused by errors or omissions, whether such errors or omissions result from negligence, accident, or any other cause.

The strategies and advice presented in this book are not a substitute for professional counseling or therapy. Seek guidance from qualified professionals for personalized support.

ABOUT THE BOOK

This book was a labor of love that took way too long to reach the surface, but I am grateful for the opportunity to share my experiences and insights with others going through similar journeys.

In the following chapters, we will discuss a range of topics related to deployments, including preparation and communication strategies, coping techniques for dealing with separation, deployment emotions, reunions, and tips for maintaining strong relationships amidst the challenges of military life.

Whether you are a military spouse, significant other, or family member, I hope this book can provide valuable guidance and support as you navigate the ups and downs of deployments. Understanding of the stages of deployment can help to prevent crises, minimize the need for command or mental health intervention, and can reduce suicidal ideation.

Remember, you are not alone in this journey. At some points, the journeys feels hard, but you have done hard before and you grew through those hard and challenging moments. We can make it through anything together.

Sometimes, the deployment story/reality is sad, scary, and lonely, and will test our desire and will to continue down this path.

Looking back, there is no other way I would have wanted to do the last twenty years. There were challenges, there were hardships, and our kids struggled at times, but in reality, they are much more prepared to cope with the roller coaster of this crazy world.

Let's dive in and explore the life of deployments!

CONTENTS

HOW TO USE THIS BOOK

The emotional cycle of deployment is a cycle, a series of events that happen repeatedly in the same order ("Cycle"). Understanding this cycle will help you cope, understand, react, be proactive, and increase family connection and resiliency as you progress through each step and each stage of the cycle.

With each progression of the cycle, new skills are developed. At the same time, the reactions of family members will change, requiring the development of different skills, and more compassion, grace, and understanding from the family.

Make this book your go-to reference as you navigate through life changes and endure multiple deployments. Keep in mind that life will move on, your children will grow up, and their reactions to subsequent deployments will likely be different from their reactions to the first one.

When people know what to expect, they can prepare and think through a situation, allowing them to react differently or to make a choice as to how they are going to react.

Preparing for situations gives people the power to be proactive and less reactive, supporting growth, resiliency, executive brain functioning, crisis survival skills, positive relationships, and overall well-being.

As a military spouse, you need to understand the unique challenges that come with this lifestyle. That's why I wrote this book: to offer guidance and support from someone who's been there. As a fellow military spouse, mom, and therapist, I know what it takes to thrive in this role. There are lot of different ways to thrive in this role and this stage of life. My way may not be your way and that is okay. Use your own discernment. When there is a question, seek out the answer. You may find that there are many solutions to the question, but again, that is where your discretion comes in play.

This book is for you, to help you navigate the ups and downs of military life with confidence and resilience. By understanding the emotional cycle of deployment and its impact on military families, you can gain greater insight into the challenges you and your loved ones may face.

This understanding will help you develop effective strategies to cope with each stage. Eventually, you will be able to anticipate the reactions of your children, understand their emotional cycles, and help them build the resilience they will need to navigate life's challenges.

Each deployment and each stage is different for everyone; understanding and familiarizing yourself with the cycles will help you better cope with your emotions and understand your family's behavior. Understanding what to expect from family members can lead to better communication and more enjoyable interactions.

Understanding that your emotions and feelings will undergo significant changes with every deployment is crucial. It is important to recognize that when your feelings don't match how you think you should feel or are vastly different from previous work ups or deployments, you should not shame or blame yourself. There is a good chance that your reactions are going to be different each time.

Let me repeat that because it is an important piece of continuous deployments. If your feelings don't match how you think you should feel or are vastly different from previous deployments it is *okay* and *normal*. Don't let your self-talk shame or blame you.

> Providing information about what to expect, especially to families who have not endured a lengthy separation before, can go a long way towards "normalizing" and coping positively with the deployment experience. Furthermore, promoting understanding of the stages helps to avert crises. (Pincus et al.)

OVERVIEW

Welcome to this life guide on military deployments, where I hope you can find valuable knowledge and support. As someone who has experienced being on the home front of multiple combat deployments, I understand the struggles and challenges that come with this lifestyle. I also know that it is 100 percent worth it.

My name is Allison, and I am a spouse of a former active-duty sailor who has since retired. Together, we have navigated the rough waters of the emotional cycle of deployment while building a home and raising a family. In addition, I discovered who I was and wanted to become within the mix.

The waters were not always calm, and a lot of the time, I wondered if I could tread any longer or if I would begin to drown. What would it mean if I stayed and what it would mean for my family if I gave up and left this lifestyle? Would it be better for them, and for me, if we just cut our losses and stopped trying? I had many nights alone to think, reflect, and grow as a person. My conclusion was and still is that, *yes*, it was worth it.

It was worth it for my children. They grew up with a larger perspective of things in life. It was worth it for me. It made me a stronger, more resilient person. It was important for my marriage; we are stronger for it. We know what it is like to start over; it is not easy. Change for humans in general is not fun, but we can do it. We did do it—a lot—and that is an accomplishment in itself.

Two of the most common difficulties I frequently hear people express are that they lack the knowledge about how to make new friends and they find it challenging to cope with change. However, military families are accustomed to these traits and frequently encounter them, which makes them second nature.

We become what we repeatedly do.
—Sean Covey (Covey 2015)

BUILDING ON EXPERIENCE AND KNOWLEDGE IN THERAPY

As a seasoned therapist (that is so strange to write) with over two decades of experience, I have worked in a variety of settings, such as rehabilitation centers for adolescents, domestic violence shelters, state psychiatric hospitals, drug and alcohol centers, and private practice. Throughout my career, I have also had the privilege of counseling and coaching active-duty service members and their families.

My experience has allowed me to understand various therapy theories and techniques deeply. I am certified in multiple approaches and continuously strive to expand my knowledge and skills in the field. A running joke is that certifications are my trauma response. I believe that we are always doing the best we can at any given time, and we can do better. Sometimes my best is 10 percent, and I am going to give it every bit of that 10 percent I can. Sometimes my best is 50 percent or 100 percent. On those days, I do better because I have more to give. I am also a mom battling with lupus, high blood pressure, weight, and all of the other things that zap our energy and get in the way of giving 100 percent every day to everything. It is important to notice and pay attention to how your best varies every day and respect your bodies for that. Our brains and bodies are protecting us, but we have to be mindful not to use and abuse them because we can injure them.

I use analogies and metaphors a lot. Think of your body as a car and your brain as the engine. You can't drive far or fast on a flat tire, and if you put the wrong kind of oil or gas in, the car will not work. That means take care of your body; self-care is maintenance. What you eat and drink is fuel for your engine, your brain. We all have a gut metabolism and a brain metabolism, and if you want your body to run smoothly, make wise decisions and take care of them.

One area to which I have dedicated a significant portion of my career is helping military families understand military-specific life challenges and heal from trauma. This type of work requires specialized training and a great deal of empathy, compassion, and patience. I am thankful to have been able to support numerous individuals on their path toward healing and growth. This book is not an alternative to therapy. It is for informational purposes only; use it to help you understand and gain compassion. Seek professional advice from someone who can take the time to get to know you and your family dynamics and help in times of need.

We can't direct the wind, but we can adjust the sails.
—Thomas S. Monson (Monson 2012)

THE CHALLENGES OF BEING
A MILITARY SPOUSE

Being married to someone in the military means constantly adapting to new environments, schedules, and routines. It also means facing long periods of separation during deployments, training, and assignments.

There were times when I felt heartbroken, sad, and even a bit lost. These emotions are universal, but not everyone can empathize with them because they cannot fathom being in the same situation. That is why it is so important to have community. Create your community wherever you move. If you have never lived on base, move on base and make friends with the other spouses. If you don't live on base but have a strong community, friend group, book club, or mom group, stay there. If not, find one. Community and friends are going to be important, especially when you are used to having another adult to talk to for a different perspective.

In 2005, we were stationed at NAS Sigonella, Italy. That is where I met my best friend, Lindsay. You will read all about how we supported each other and helped each other through some tough times, even when we were states away. I remember when we were stationed in Virginia in 2007 or 2008. She was stationed in Florida, and our husbands were deployed. They were not deployed together, but they were deployed at the same time. We talked on the phone all the time. I remember folding laundry and watching *16 and Pregnant*—that was a part of my routine. We would also talk about *American Idol* and being moms; we supported each other from a distance.

Then, our husbands returned, and we did not talk as much, and the cycle went on. It is still going on, even though our husbands have retired. We are still good friends.

I remember the heart-wrenching anguish of our first deployment. Our son, Carson, was three years old. Carson and I flew to California to stay with my mom while my husband, Derek, was deployed. We thought it would be easier to be in a different place. Carson struggled with the workups and whenever Derek left. In his toddler mind, he was convinced Daddy was playing hide-and-seek, and we would spend days looking for him.

It was heartbreaking, and I did not want our son to go through that. I wanted him to develop relationships with his extended family. I thought it was a win-win, and looking back, it was. I love that our kids have such a strong relationship with extended family.

However, that was the most challenging flight and deployment to prepare for. As we walked down the tarmac, I fought tears. I knew we didn't break up, that it was just another deployment, and I had so much to be grateful for. Still, in those moments, my emotions were stronger than my reasoning, and as soon as I sat down and got Carson settled, I lost it.

I could not fight the tears; it felt like we broke up. It felt like my heart had broken into a million pieces. It hurt—it literally felt like I had a hole in my heart.

Here's a little scientific fact: our emotions can turn on our pain receptors, literally causing us pain.

Think about that for a minute. Our emotions are so strong we feel physical pain. Our emotions are not rational and sometimes don't fit the situation, but the feelings are so real, so big, they cause pain and exhaustion, and can make us sick.

It is important in those moments to acknowledge the pain and cry but not to get lost in it. What helped me was focusing on my personal goals and my self-improvement. I would tell myself that this is the deployment, and I am going to get toned and healthy, save some amount of money, or do a project. Sometimes I accomplished it, and sometimes I didn't, but the important thing is that I was working toward bettering myself.

Change and deployments can take a toll on one's mental and emotional well-being. The fear of the unknown, the constant worry for our loved one's safety, and the sense of isolation from family and friends can sometimes be overwhelming, but it is what you make it.

Acknowledge the hurt, fear, and chaos, embrace it, and decide to do something else. Sometimes all you have to do is decide to do something to change your emotional state.

On another note, gratitude is the first step to developing compassion. It is not selfish; it is kind.

Starting a habit of journaling about gratitude is a good idea.

Coping Techniques

To help myself manage these challenges, I have turned to various resources such as cognitive behavior therapy (CBT) and dialectical behavior therapy (DBT). These techniques and the development of community have provided me with practical tools to cope with stress, anxiety, and other difficult emotions.

Additionally, I have also created my own "deployment checklist," which includes self-care practices, emergency contacts, and important documents that helped me feel more prepared for my spouse's deployments.

My story is not unique, but it is a testament to the strength, resilience, and courage that all military spouses possess. It is my hope that by sharing my journey, others will feel less alone and more empowered to face the challenges of being military spouses.

Remember that you are not alone on this journey, and there are always resources and support available to help you through it all. Stay strong, stay grateful, and stay compassionate.

I am sitting at my computer, taking a deep breath and a sip of tea, and preparing to be vulnerable with you, my fellow military spouses. I encourage you to grab a cup of coffee or tea, get comfortable, and join me. As you read this book, I hope parts of the story will be like watching a reality TV show; you sit back, enjoy your drink, and comment in your head or aloud as the story unfolds.

In this book, I will not only share personal stories and theories but will also delve into the subject of navigating through life in the military. Military life is an exceptional experience that comes with its own set of challenges, sacrifices, and opportunities for growth and development.

One significant but often overlooked aspect of military life is the impact on family members, especially spouses who stay behind while their loved ones deploy to distant and often dangerous locations. This book aims to shed light on the struggles and triumphs of military families and provide insight into the inner workings of the military itself.

I invite you to join me in exploring the uncharted territories of military life, to better comprehend what it truly means to serve and sacrifice for one's country. Thank you for embarking on this journey with me, and I look forward to navigating these stories together. So grab your favorite beverage, and let's continue our adventure.

PUBLISHED FACTS ABOUT MILITARY FAMILIES

These facts were easy to find on the website dosomething.org.

Since 2001, more than two-million American children have had a parent deploy at least once.

More than 900,000 children have experienced the deployments of one or both parents on multiple occasions.

Military families relocate 10 times or more often than civilian families—on average they relocate every two to three years.

Children in military families experience a high rate of mental health, trauma, and related problems. About 30% reported feeling sad and hopeless almost every day for two weeks during the last 12 months. Nearly one in four reported having considered suicide. ("11 Facts about Military Families")

MY STORY
~ THE BEGINNING ~

Welcome to the life of deployments. I was a military spouse, and my husband retired from twenty years of active duty in 2019. For sixteen years, I was a military spouse, mother, daughter, sister, and aunt trying to navigate the military lifestyle healthily in an uncertain world.

I am now a therapist with more than two decades of experience counseling, coaching, and supporting active-duty service members and their family members. (That sounds so strange to write about me, but it is true, and I am proud of it). I have worked in rehabilitation centers for adolescents, domestic violence shelters, state psychiatric hospitals, and private practice. I am certified in various therapy techniques and have spent much of my life helping people heal from trauma. All trauma is distressing, and the families living in and supporting this lifestyle are not acknowledged for the traumas that impact us.

From my experience, when people try to reach out for support, they are met with, "Well, you signed up for this life" or "Put your big girl panties on." At first, this was offensive. It made me feel weak and like I was less than or not good enough. However, I realized that most people don't know how to help or what to say to encourage you. They are new to this, too.

My story might sound like yours or that of someone you know. You understand somewhat where I come from and can picture my story and my experiences. Therefore, we can develop rapport and maybe you can laugh, learn something to watch out for, or adopt coping skills or techniques I listed in the appendix. After all, I am not so different from the average military spouse.

As you read this book, I hope that you become invested in the story. I hope you can relate to the stages, can picture a friend, family member, or yourself experiencing these events and stages, or can picture situations that are similar. That is my hope anyway, and it would be a sign that we are making a connection. You are invested in learning and watching this book's stories, theories, and skills as you read the pages, making it more likely that you will be able to recall the information when or should you need it.

I met my husband when we were in high school. I was fifteen, and he was sixteen; we hung out with the same friends. We were never more than friends, and it aggravated me when he would swing by my house unannounced. He frequently did that because it annoyed me.

I was a teenage girl and needed and wanted to be prepared for company. Remember, people don't necessarily like change or surprises, and when he decided to drop by unexpectedly, I was usually doing something. Back then, I rollerbladed and exercised a lot. I loved Billy Blanks Tae Bo workouts and did not like looking messy and unprepared. I lived in a house on a golf course with a pool. It was a great house in Palm Desert, California. Let me go back a little further so I can paint the picture of how this all began. Fate played a role in our story.

Between the ages of five and fourteen, I was raised in LaQuinta, California. It is more of a city now, but this took place before it was built up, in the late 1980s. After my first year in high school, when I was fourteen, my mom, brothers, and I moved to Massachusetts. That is where my grandparents, aunts, cousins, and all my mom's family lived. My dad and mom's relationship was not good. Not good is an understatement; it was downright dysfunctional.

That move was short-lived because my family moved back to California eight months later. We were renting a house from one of my mom's friends in Palm Desert. For those of you who don't know the Coachella Valley, LaQuinta, and Palm Desert, neighboring cities, and rival schools, because our house was in Palm Desert, I had to go to Palm Desert High School while all my friends were twenty minutes away at LaQuinta High School. Of course, I wanted to return to La Quinta to continue and graduate with the friends I started kindergarten with, but for then, I had to attend Palm Desert High.

This put me in the middle of my sophomore year. That is where I met Derek. We had some classes together, and at lunch, we all ate at the same tree in the quad.

Our love story was inspired by fate. I moved houses in Palm Desert once, and my mom eventually bought a home in the La Quinta High School zone. That was senior year and I returned to La Quinta High School. Derek moved to a different high school too, graduated early, and joined the Navy in 1999. I graduated in 2000.

At that time, we ran into each other by what appeared to be a coincidence. Once, in late 1999 or 2000, before school was out, he was back and just so happened to drive down the street I lived on (this was a different house than the pool house), and I just so happened to be outside. We hung out for a few days, and I helped him find gifts for his girlfriend and plan romantic dates for them. I lost contact again for a while. In the summer of 2001, he was visiting home and called my pager a few times but never left a callback number.

I remember it was summer because I spent the summers of 2000 and 2001 at my grandparents' house in Massachusetts, working as a camp counselor at the Cape Cod Sea Camp. I called a mutual friend, Pat, to ask if he had Derek's contact information because Derek never left a callback number. Derek answered the phone.

We reconnected as friends and eventually fell in love through letters sent in the mail during his second deployment. That was one of the deployments at the beginning of the Iraq war; his deployment was delayed and turned around a few times. They called it the shock and awe deployment. He did romantic things like painting my name on one of the missiles and sending me pictures. They spent Christmas in port in Australia that year. If I remember correctly, they came home in the late summer.

I went with his mom, dad, and sister to pick him up at the pier in San Diego. I remember those dates because it was right before my twenty-first birthday. Derek, his mom, dad, sister, and I drove from the pier to Lake Havasu, Arizona, for some rest and relaxation. The first night, we were at the bar in the desert, and his mom announced my birthday was in a few days. That was a fun night, a fun trip, and the beginning of Derek and me being more than friends.

It was big news that this deployment was over, and the local news was there. Everyone was there; it was called a deployment fair. Families lined the peers, waiting for their service members to walk off the carrier. The service members lined the deck in their dress whites as the larger-than-life ship slowly pulled in. There were welcome signs, parades, people dressed up, vendors' booths, banks, car dealers, raffles, and local and national news stations. His dad was interviewed on the nightly news that day. The reporter asked about who was in our party holding signs, and there was a joke because he said I was a friend, which I was. The news reporter said something like, "You know, that is a good dad; he is not committing his son to a relationship." It was clever and funny, but really, we were just friends then.

I was a preschool teacher and a college student at the local community college back then, but we spent all our time together. When he had to return to base, we visited each other on the weekends. At one point, I remember him talking about being up for orders and listing NAS Sigonella as one of the options. It was a great idea. We didn't know what he would get, and I believe in fate. A few months later, when I was working, he called. I stepped into the bathroom to take the call, and he said, "We got orders to Italy." He was so excited, and I remember feeling so excited for him. At the same time, I knew I was not moving to another country unless I was married.

We talked about it. He knew I would visit him, but I could not move to another country and not be protected legally. It would be a better move on my end if we were married.

We had time, and I would not push him, but I was not moving with him.

Derek reenlisted on the previous deployment and got a lot of money that he used to buy a Jeep Rubicon. I would go to the Jeep dealers with him, and more than once, the salesperson would ask him if he needed to talk it over with his wife or ask, "Does your wife like it?" We would laugh and brush it off.

Then I went with him to look at apartments. He had a friend he worked with, and they would be roommates. The apartment clerks would also refer to me as his wife; we just laughed and said that no, I was not his wife.

He understood where I came from, not wanting to leave the country and live on a military base without any rights.

We broke up for two weeks and got back together. That was hard. We lived six hours apart, but I was so used to talking to him daily. He was my best friend even back then.

I have always had good intuition and understanding of why people do what they do. I did not know what he was doing while we were broken up, but I knew he was torn because he loved me. He didn't want to admit it to himself. That was also confirmed when we got back together.

Still, we knew the day was coming and didn't know what would happen to us.

He proposed one weekend; he was visiting, and I was not feeling well. He walked into my room while I was folding laundry, holding a ring.

I should have known what it was for, but I didn't, and I asked if he was proposing. In my defense, he gave me a diamond "friendship" ring on our first Christmas while we were dating. I was so confused. His intention with present giving is somewhat confusing.

He asked my mom for her blessing and talked to his parents, and I had no idea. He still surprises me sometimes.

We had to be married quickly because I had to be on his orders to go to Italy with him, so we had a small wedding in Las Vegas, Nevada at the Little White Wedding Chapel. It was just us, and it was great. Then, a few months later, we had a big Catholic wedding with friends and family.

I know many military spouses have similar stories because the legal paperwork must be taken care of by a specific time. Most of the time, they need it before you even know they need it. I am sharing all of this to help new spouses and people not affiliated with military family culture understand some cultural norms.

Fast forward a few years, and we had our first child in Italy, our second in Virginia, and our third in California. The entire time, I worked, went to school, raised my family, and supported my husband through military deployments and military stuff. It wasn't easy, but it was what needed to be done. I was determined not to become a negative statistic, and as I grew and matured, it became my goal to inform spouses of the cycles and statistics, too. I wanted spouses to know they could make a choice, be informed, and know they were in control of their lives while belonging to the United States military.

That was the beginning of my life experience as a military spouse. This book is a complete account of my lived experiences and what I learned about the emotional cycle of deployment. This is, in my opinion, the number one thing military families need to understand.

As you go through this book, you can implement everything you learn immediately and have a more robust understanding of the emotional reactions your family experiences. This can give you a new perspective on their behaviors and can change how you interact and relate daily.

Life begins at the end of your comfort zone.
—Mel Robbins (Robbins)

CHAPTER 1

What Is a Deployment?

Merriam-Webster's dictionary defines a deployment as a "placement or arrangement (as of military personnel or equipment) in position for a particular use or purpose; an instance of such placement (as in a battle zone) for a period of time" ("Deployment").

My simplified definition is that deployment is a lengthy separation from the family unit for a specified time frame. This can be a difficult experience for military families. It can cause physical, emotional, and psychological stress. Deployment can also have an impact on the dynamics of relationships within the family, as well as on the mental health of the individual members.

Military families are not the only ones that experience deployments. Families of truckers, firefighters, and businesspeople or anyone who routinely spends time away from the primary family unit experience deployment. This book references the military and armed services deployments because this is my experience. The statistics surrounding deployments are alarming. I will give my beliefs as a professional, spouse, and mother who has lived the military lifestyle. The numbers are a lot higher than reported.

I worked on three bases as a military work and family life counselor for years. I can't give you a number of how many marriages struggled or broke up, or one party had a psychological emergency, but it was *a lot*.

Back then, I didn't keep track; I was immersed in living the cycle. I was trying to make sure that my family was not one of the negative statistics. I was doing what I could to support my family, and to try to hold my stuff together for my family and the families I served.

Yes, spouses serve, too, and our jobs are just as important as the service members' jobs. Without us, they wouldn't be so determined to make it home. I am a strength-based, dialectical behavior therapist. I honestly believe people are always doing their best with the life skills they have available to them at that moment. Our best changes from day to day. Some days our best is 100% percent and some days our best is 10 percent. On the days when my best is 100 percent, you bet I operate and give every bit of that 100 percent to life. On days where my best is 10 percent, I give my day and family every bit of that 10 percent.

Okay, let me try to explain it like this. I am dyslexic. I was diagnosed when I was six or seven. Reading and writing has always been a challenge for me. Some days, I catch my mistakes and correct them on the spot and some days, I don't even notice them (neither does Microsoft Word). That doesn't change the fact that I did my best. My best is just different from day to day.

I have been in the counseling community in every state my family lived in. I focused on family issues, adolescent counseling, domestic violence issues, drug and alcohol abuse, adolescents and adults within the criminal system, adolescent and adult in-patient rehabilitation, and psychiatric hospitals. I have lived worldwide and can tell you I don't believe the statistics are correct.

I can tell you that more than six of my son's friends have committed suicide. The youngest child I saw who tried to commit suicide was five years old. There are reports of children writing suicide notes and wishing they "were not alive" from the first grade on.

With my son's friends, the suicides happened during middle school and high school. Each one was a shock. No one would have guessed that these kids would decide to take their own lives. Some of them happened while a parent was deployed, some happened while their parents were divorcing, and some happened once the family retired from the military. Their socioeconomic factors were all different; their genders and cultures were also different. There were no commonalities other than the military affiliation. These were normal kids hiding an immense amount of pain and hiding it well for a long time, until it became too much for them to bear.

The five-year-old wanted to be with the deployed parent and the parent at home was distraught over the deployment too. Once the attempt was made, it was an eye opener for the parent and they both got help.

These are numbers that you will never forget because of the impact they have on the community and family as a whole.

I know that my husband has been affected by a few military suicides of people in his command and on a deployment with him. He told me about a friend in another command on the same deployment. He knew something was wrong when he walked by this friend and said, "Hi." My husband talked vaguely about the emptiness in his friend's eyes, and that he wished he asked what wrong sooner was. He had dreams about this event and sometimes still does. His friend had four kids and a wife at home.

He has lost more than one friend on deployments due to suicide. These just the ones that stand out to me because I knew them or knew their families and their stories stuck with me. They affected me and helped me understand my husband and his reaction to adverse happenings better.

One of his last duties for his military career was to go into the apartment of one of his shipmates who committed suicide. The apartment was still soaked with blood. My husband went into the apartment to retrieve the cat for his friend's girlfriend. The girlfriend was also a shipmate in the same command; she lived in the apartment with the friend who committed suicide. The girlfriend was away on a detachment when it happened.

My husband told me about the cat having blood on its nose and he wanted to clean the cat before giving it back to the girlfriend.

The guy and the girl were both in his command, and he was close friends with both of them. That event alone was pretty traumatic.

Facing just one of those traumas is enough to put people into a tailspin of destruction.

Now add all the things that military members face and all the significant life events that their families face: all the moves, buying and selling property, starting new schools, and new carriers. It becomes easy to see why there is a stigma around military families.

Military families know how to start over, compartmentalize, and get through living in high-stress environments. This is great because it often helps families develop the resilience to survive in fast-paced, high-stress environments. However, it can also be seen as a negative because it means that military families are at a higher risk of divorce, suicide, addictions, and some other negative statistics. Learning about the cycles and being sensitive to the trauma, also referred to as being trauma-informed, is the first step.

I can tell you how intimately knowing the people who passed and caring for the people left affected my son, husband, and family.

I can tell you that I was aware of the risks. I paid attention and looked for signs, and still couldn't protect my family from all the abuses and trauma in the world.

I can tell you that my husband did not react well, and we separated at one point. Once, he put the barrel of a gun in his mouth; luckily, he stopped. He made a different choice. He credits our dog for saving his life because the dog snapped him out of the negative spiral long enough for him to make another choice.

I am one person, and my family and I experienced these statistics. There is nothing exceptional about my life or the life my family and I live. We are good, normal, everyday people and that was my experience.

I believe that the rates are *a lot* higher. The people I knew who committed suicide did not display any of the classic red flags, and lots of people in the community were completely blindsided.

It is better to be safe than sorry.

Isn't that why we are told to prepare for emergencies and have routine earthquake, fire, and active shooter drills in schools and businesses? These events that every family needs to be ready for because it can mean the difference between life and death, and they are outside of our control.

Military families need to understand the emotional cycle of deployment and its impact on their lives.

> Knowing what you need to do to improve your life takes wisdom. Pushing yourself to do it takes courage.
>
> —Mel Robbins (Robbins)

WHAT MILITARY DEPLOYMENT CAN LOOK LIKE

The emotional cycle of deployment involves the physical and emotional separation of loved ones during deployment. It is a process of mourning for the loss of a loved one, adjusting to his or her absence, then readjusting to the person's return. This process can be a roller coaster of emotions, ranging from sadness and loneliness to pride and joy. During this cycle, families must learn to cope with the separation, adjust to the new normal, and find ways to stay connected with their loved ones, and then reconnect when they return to do it all over again in a specific amount of time.

My experience is with navy deployments, but there are a lot of different deployments. The division and service type of the deploying spouse deploying may be different, but the stages and emotions you and your family experience will be the similar. Here is a helpful link that will help you narrow down what your service member's deployment may look like: https://www.military.com/deployment/deployment-overview.html.

The deployment cycle starts as soon as you learn about the possibility of the deployment. Little separations occur before the deployment. Called workups, these are little separations working up to the main event, also known as the deployment.

For my husband, it looked like this: three weeks gone, ten days home, followed by four weeks gone, ten days home, one month gone, ten to fifteen days home, three months gone, and ten to fifteen days home leading to a six-month deployment.

When they return from deployment, they will be home between three and six months, and then it will start again for the duration of the sea duty cycle. The length of the sea duty cycle is different for everyone, depending on the person's job and what he or she works on. My family's rotation was four and a half years of sea duty and two to three years of shore duty.

Shore duty meant that he didn't deploy but still participated in training and short separations, training exercises, or recertification in preparation for the deployment cycle. Sometimes, there was an exceptional circumstance or he needed to do something else, such as fix a broken jet, which I did not consider an emergency but the military did.

Being flexible with plans is a necessity. When planning, you need to consider at least three variations. What actually happens will more than likely be a combination of all three.

I advise people to have a plan A, B, and C. The variation would be a combination of A and C with a hint of D. Being able to roll with the punches is a lifestyle. It becomes second nature. At times, it is sort of exhilarating, like being on the Indiana Jones ride at Disneyland or on a roller coaster. The excitement builds as you climb. You enjoy the quick turns and small drops. Then, there is the big drop, the one you have been preparing for, and you hold on for dear life hoping the seat restraints don't fail. You depend on the roller coaster to land safely. Then, you catch your breath just to get in line and do it all over again.

As far as the family was concerned, shore duty was a time to concentrate on family relationships and schedule family vacations, reintegrate the service member back into the family unit, bond as a family unit, and fall in love again. Most importantly, it was a time to make lasting memories.

The need for my husband to leave on an emergency navy jet retrieval operation has only happened to my family once that I can remember. We were living in Virginia at the time. It was late May, so the weather was hot. I was nine months pregnant, my in-laws came to visit from California, and our son was turning five. My husband promised me he would be home, so we invited the entire preschool class to the birthday party. I was shocked that everyone planned on attending. Two or three days into my in-laws' visit, my husband was sent to another state on "emergency jet retrieval." From what I remember, it was nothing big and not an emergency, but the command wanted the jet back as soon as possible.

My husband left on what should have been a quick overnight trip. Nothing is as easy as it seems, and he was gone for over a week. During that time, I nine months was pregnant, the weather was hot, my in-laws were visiting, and I was hosting a birthday party for twenty kids.

I love my in-laws. I was blessed with an amazing extended family, but I felt awkward at that point in my life. I imagine that parts of that stay were strange for my in laws too; they go to visit their son and are left with his pregnant wife, five-year-old son, and a birthday party. They are pretty great grandparents, and I was used to the awkward feelings of attending family gatherings with my husband's family without my husband.

Embrace the awkwardness. It builds character, or at least that is what I told myself. It helped.

I am a planner and plan for the just-in-case scenario. Once you have been a part of the military lifestyle for a few years, you'll realize that the just-in-case scenarios happen more than you desire. Anyway, I had planned to have the party at one of the activity trampoline venues. It took a lot of planning because I had to reserve the party venue months in advance and save money. After all, those parties are more expensive than a home party, but I knew I would be nine months pregnant, and I did not want the stress of hosting a party at our house.

Fast forward seven years, and I had three children: a twelve-year-old boy, a seven-year-old girl, and a two-year-old girl. My husband had seniority and had been on active duty for nineteen years. He was not due to go on a workup for three weeks. It was June in California, and we had a house with a pool. Our seven-year-old wanted a pool party with her friends. We had been at that base for four years, and the kids had developed close friends, so I planned a pool party. I was expecting between fourteen and seventeen kids. My husband would be there so we could grill and socialize with the parents. We already knew most of the parents because that base was small, and my husband worked with some of them.

My husband was told two days before the party that he needed to go to the boat to prepare for the rest of the command to arrive. I thought he had three weeks before he had to go.

I am not a gambler, but I would have bet on him being home if I were. Luckily, I also had some wonderful friends who helped me. We ended up having a wonderful time. The girls made slime, ate pizza, swam, and hit a piñata. The party was so much fun, and I have many good memories. The kids still talk about the piñata that hung from the chandelier under the awning in the backyard. One piece of advice I have is that if you are planning a kid's birthday party or a big event, don't count on your service member attending. Then, if he or she is able to attend, it is a huge bonus and an extra set of hands, and you are not left breaking hearts and scrambling for more help.

More on Deployment

As a fellow military spouse, I can tell you my husband has deployed nine times in nineteen years. Sometimes, the deployments were back-to-back, meaning he didn't get the three to six months to be at home to focus on work and family. He came home for a month before all the workups started again.

The work-up cycle I described is for a six-month deployment. We have only had one six-month deployment; the other deployments were between eight and twelve months. I am adding my experience with time frames for planning purposes. I am so grateful that my spouse made it back, and my heart goes out to the families of the service members who have not made it back. You are still part of the military family, and we will always have your back.

Thank you to the service members and the families who supported and loved them; their sacrifices were not in vain.

Looking at this from a therapist's point of view, it is no wonder why the divorce rate, suicide rate, and child abuse rates are so high.

While we are on the topic of stress, no military book would be complete without a topic on Murphy and his fabulous law. Murphy's Law is an epigram that states, "Anything that can go wrong will go wrong," and that is true during a deployment. My advice is that when this happens, breathe and look at it as the universe testing your patience and strength. You will make it through whatever happens and someday laugh at it.

Ready for some of my Murphy's Law stories?

When we lived in Nevada, I would drive from Fallon, Nevada to La Quinta, California with a seven-year-old, a two-year-old and a small dog often. It was a nine hour and twenty-five minute drive according to Map Quest. With one adult, two kids, and a small dog it, was more like eleven hours. I would drive it in one sitting, stopping once at a McDonald's in Hawthorn and along the side of the road along the grapevine. I should say the goal was to stop once. If I had to stop, it was at least a thirty-minute delay. I wanted to be efficient, so I prepared with drinks, snacks, and diapers. I didn't eat or drink much so I wouldn't have to stop and navigate going to the bathroom with two little kids in a gas station. I probably made that trip ten to fifteen times.

Once, I blew a tire between Hawthorn and Ridgecrest, California. There was nothing around. It is a desolate area. There was storm a few hours behind me and I had to pull over on the side of 395, empty my trunk to get to my spare tire, and read the directions on how to change it. Eventually, a police officer stopped and asked if he could help. I think he must have felt bad because I was obviously struggling, it was windy, and I had the directions out trying to change my tire. The officer was nice and told me to hurry to Ridgecrest, which was a few hours away, because there was one shop that might have a tire that could work. He was not confident there would be a tire on hand the other store and I definitely could not make it back to Fallon on a spare. It was at least six or seven hours away in the dark. I am not afraid of the dark, but the roads would be frozen and that would be unsafe.

I made it to the shop in Ridgecrest right before it closed. Along the way, I was pulled over by a different police officer who wanted to know why I was driving so slowly. I was *done*! The officer looked at my spare tire and let me go warning me to be careful because a storm was coming.

Ridgecrest is small town; they didn't have a tire that would work but they had another car with the size tire I needed in the yard. They changed my tire and I checked into a hotel for the night. I remember everyone giving me suggestions on times to leave to beat the second part of the storm so I was not stuck for a few days. I don't remember how big the storm was. I remember it was rainy and windy and it snowed.

Another time, I was making the same trip with the same small children and dog. It was July 3. I was in the fast lane driving through Los Angeles. I started to smell brakes or something. All of a sudden, my car started smoking and the temperature gauge went to H. I put my blinker on and made it through the off ramp, coming to a stop on the side of a busy street on a holiday weekend in over 100-degree heat. I called the tow truck and we waited for seven hours. I was pouring water on the kids' heads to keep them cool. A trucker stopped in the middle of the street and gave us extra water. Apparently, there is a piece that links the radiator with three other pieces of the car, and it blew. Not a quick fix. My brother picked us up and we stayed at his house in Fountain Valley. My in-laws picked us up the next day. The car was in the shop for a week. They drove us back to Los Angeles to get the car and we drove back to Fallon.

Now that I think of it, that car had a lot of issues. It would randomly decide not to start but it was not the battery or alternator. I would take it to the shop and magically it would work. (That is an example of Murphy's Law.)

I turned that car in and got a new Honda Odyssey. My Odyssey is more than ten years old, and I still love it.

Enough car stories. Let me introduce you to Murphy and house maintenance.

We bought a wonderful house in Lemoore, California. It is my favorite house, and the one where my daughter had her pool party. At that time, I had a sixth grader, a first grader, a two-year-old, and two dogs. I was cleaning the house and doing laundry. The kids were just being kids doing what they do best: not cleaning.

I was expecting the refrigerator repairman because the freezer would not stay cold. Apparently, I left a broom outside by the front door.

The repairman arrived and rang the door. I answered it and he came in. While I was talking to the repairman, he informed me that when he services houses for military families and there is a broom outside the front door, it means he is servicing more than just the refrigerator, if you know what I mean. That was a huge misunderstanding. I was mortified. I really only needed him to fix the freezer. While he was telling me this and I was turning red, the dog went through the trash. My son blamed it on the two-year-old. I noticed that one of those little moisture prevention pouches was open on the floor, and there were little beads scattered everywhere. I thought that my two-year-old just ate God knows what because my son blamed the trash on the floor on her. Long story short, my son was afraid I was going to get rid of the dog if the dog made another mess. I probably did say that this dog was bad.

At that point, I was on the phone with poison control and investigating the trash. The TV was blaring in the living room. The repairman thought he was getting more than he was. The laundry was overflowing out of the laundry room, and the dishwasher exploded water all over the kitchen. It was not a leak; it was a wave from the bottom of the dishwasher.

Murphy's Law is really about everyday things that sometimes don't go as planned. However, when your spouse is gone, it intensifies the mishaps. Cortisol flows and the fight-or-flight response kicks in. Hopefully, you can laugh at Murphy when he visits because he will, sooner or later. Those become the stories of strength, resilience, and patience that build character.

CHAPTER 2

Impact of Deployment on the Family Unit

The youngest person I have personally worked with who tried to commit suicide during deployment season was five years old. We need to instill resilience and show our children that, in hard times, you get support, you learn how to adapt, and you learn that it is okay to reach out for help. At the back of this book, there is a list of helpful resources in the appendix.

The impact of deployment on military families can be significant. Families may experience various emotions, from fear and anxiety to pride and joy. They may also experience financial hardships due to decreased income or increased expenses related to deployment. The separation can also lead to feelings of isolation and conflict among family members adjusting to the new normal. Everyone in the family is affected and will react differently. I will do my best to cover the common reactions based on age, gender, number of deployments, neurodivergent family members, pets, and extended family members. Hopefully, stories from my BFF Lindsay can fill in the holes or areas where I don't have experiences. I hope you can relate to them because her family makeup and lived experiences are different from mine. Lindsay has two wonderful boys who are autistic. Her husband was deployed at similar times as mine, although not on the same deployment.

Lindsay and I walked similar parallel paths, but she has a lot of excellent knowledge to add. She had to learn how to navigate the Exceptional Family Member Program (EFMP) and advocate for her children's needs with little to no support. I have to brag a bit because when the children were not receiving proper care from the San Diego Unified School District, she sued and won twice, getting her children into a school that recognized and supported her children's needs.

Added Extra Support Resources

As an added extra, I am going to include a section before the appendix where I introduce some dialectical behavior skills to build resiliency and develop new coping techniques in mindfulness, distress tolerance, and emotional regulation.

Understanding the emotional reunion and challenges after deployment can be as challenging as the separation. After being apart for an extended period of time, it is important to take time to reconnect and reestablish the relationship. It is also important to be mindful of the individual's mental health, as he or she may be dealing with the long-term effects of deployment.

The impact of deployment on intimate relationships can be significant. Intimate relationships may suffer due to the separation and the stress of adapting to post-deployment life. It is important to be mindful of the individual's mental health and seek support from friends, family members, and organizations.

The long-term effects of deployment on mental health can vary from person to person. It is important to be aware of the signs of mental health issues, such as depression, anxiety, and post-traumatic stress disorder. It is also important to seek out professional help if needed.

(If the stages turn abusive to anyone involved, seek professional help from a chaplain, counselor, or someone who can listen, understand, and have a safety plan.) Remember the Suicide Hotline number is 988. Keep it posted so anyone can access it.

Deployment can be a challenging experience for military families, but it can also be a rewarding one that helps your family develop unrelenting strength, flexibility, determination, and perseverance to withstand whatever life throws their way.

> Remember the struggle you're facing today develops
> the strength you need for tomorrow.
>
> —Robert Tew

CHAPTER 3

Introduction to the Cycle and Stages

As I sit here writing, it is 12:19 p.m. I am so in love with my husband and so thankful for all our struggles. They formed us into the strong individuals we are today, who make one kick-ass family. It has taken us time to get here, and it pains me to write this, but our relationship was not always this strong. To get the most out of this cycle, we need to be honest and vulnerable; I will do just that because I genuinely believe that our challenges are meant to teach lessons.

As one of my friends and mentors, Desiree Dunbar, says, "Your mess is your message."

Deployment is a unique experience for military families. It is filled with mixed emotions, and the emotional cycle of deployment can have a profound impact on the well-being of military families. As a military spouse, you may feel overwhelmed, anxious, and scared as you face deployment challenges. You are not alone. This book is written to provide insight into the emotional cycle of deployment and its impact on military family members of all ages and their pets, too.

You will learn about and understand the emotional cycle of deployment. Three deployment stages and seven steps make up the cycle. The cycle begins with *pre-deployment,* followed by *deployment* and *post-deployment life.*

We will discuss the impact of deployment on intimate relationships, the long-term effects on mental health, and communication strategies during deployment. You will also understand the importance of self-care and resilience during this difficult time.

> The closer you come to understanding each cycle and its side effects, the closer you come to changing certain aspects of your life. If there is time, take part in some of the services offered to you on base. There are always people on base who can assist you. (Hochlan 2017)

Knowing what to expect will help you understand and predict your family's behavior, leading to clear, calm, supportive communication. More enjoyable interactions can assist you in identifying how or why your family members are behaving and reacting the way they are.

As a mother, I learned early on to anticipate what my children need and when they need it.

For example, when my kids were young, I would plan my day around their naps because I knew that if they were well rested, it would make the rest of our day smoother. As they got older, my expectations changed, but I knew what behaviors I could expect as we went through the day.

If I needed to take the kids with me to the grocery store and I waited until the end of the day when we were all hot, tired, and hungry, that trip would not go as planned. My children, who at the time I started writing this book were eleven, seven, and two years of age, would likely have had a fit or an argument if I tried to schlep us through a store, even if it was for something they liked because we were hot, tired, and hungry. Then, I would be agitated, anxious, and short-tempered, which would lead to comfort eating, arguments, power struggles, unhappy kids, and a stressed-out mom turned guilty mom. That isn't very pleasant and not my idea of a good time. I would rather go to the store before I get the kids from daycare or school and surprise them with the ice cream, avoiding the entire fiasco.

Unfortunately, there were times when that could not be avoided, but that was also before COVID, Instacart, and curbside pickup. Now, all these shopping conveniences are the new normal. Back when I was a solo parent, I had to be more organized and prepare my shopping list before I needed it; however, sometimes that is not reality. I still find myself making something and needing one more ingredient. That one short trip to the store with kids can take upwards of forty-five minutes. When you already feel like you are behind, it can be the beginning of the stressnado.

Places like Walmart Supercenters and Super Targets were my favorites because they were one-stop shops for food, diapers, toys, and household things, and I could have my car serviced while I shopped. Once curbside pickup became a thing, I took advantage of it. However, I would still find myself going to more stores because the store would be out of something or the staff would substitute an item with something that did not work for my plan.

Now my kids are older, but it still takes time. I will always forget an ingredient, then go to two, or need to go to two, separate grocery stores to get what I need.

Today, I opt to use a grocery meal service. I switch between the brands depending on who has the best meal plan for my diet and the best prices. I usually rotate between Blue Apron, Hello Fresh, and Home Chef. There are more out there. What is available will depend on your location. Do a Google search and ask around for the best deals around your area. I am also a fan of crock-pot meals.

I am not endorsed by any of these companies. I am just sharing my time- and stress-saving strategies.

> Change is the only constant in life. One's ability to
> adapt to those changes will determine success in life.
> —Benjamin Franklin

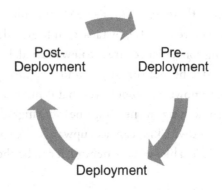

Post-Deployment   Pre-Deployment

Deployment

Each part of the cycle is broken down into stages. There are 7 steps total, and each stage corresponds with a specific part of the cycle. Please see the chart below and remember, "Acknowledging the whole range of feelings is the first step toward dealing with them in a healthy manner" (Logan 2022).

STAGE 1	Anticipation of Departure	Pre-Deployment
STAGE 2	Detachment and Withdrawal	
STAGE 3	Emotional Disorganization	Deployment
STAGE 4	Recovery and Stabilization	
STAGE 5	Anticipation of Return	
STAGE 6	Return, Adjust, Reintergrate	Post- Deployment
STAGE 7	Reintergration and Stabilization	

CHAPTER 4

Pre-Deployment

The pre-deployment cycle is commonly discussed in terms of stages accompanying each part of the cycle or each cycle stage. During the pre-deployment cycle, the main events, also known as stages, are

1. anticipation of departure; and
2. detachment and withdrawal.

Anticipation of Departure

The pre-deployment stage typically begins one to six weeks before deployment and lasts until deployment. Still, from my experience as a spouse with children, it starts as soon as your service member is told or has a timeline that the impending deployment has a date.

Once you get a date or a time frame, it makes the event appear more real and final.

For me, the grieving process and the withdrawal process overlapped. Grieving is a process, and yes, it is normal to grieve the separation of a family member.

My first emotional reaction is to cry; I am the type of person who will cry when I am sad, stressed, angry, my head hurts, or when I am tired or overwhelmed. My husband is a joker and makes jokes to handle emotional or stressful situations. The kids' reactions changed over the years, but in the beginning, they didn't understand. Developmentally, they could not plan or dream that far into the future. After I address more about the adults and the household, I will talk about the reactions that you can expect from children, with the disclaimer that each child is different and has his or her own struggles. Listen and pay attention to the kids spacing out and the kids acting out; they could both be in the middle of a trauma reaction.

As the adult responsible for caring for the home front, kids, pets, finances, and things of that nature, it is important to start planning for the service member to deploy. That means you need to logically consider the timeline plan months in advance and change how holidays are typically celebrated so the service member can spend time with the family and vice versa.

For example, if my service member were scheduled to miss Christmas, we would have a small Christmas as a family. Sometimes, that meant we had a Christmas tree up in July or October. We would talk about the events my husband would miss, but we would put a positive spin on it, do something special, and make a fantastic memory. For example, my husband missed a lot of our son's birthdays. I made it a tradition to go to SeaWorld for our son's birthday because it was something special, and military families got in free once a year. That was a huge bonus because the military family of an enlisted service member does not make much.

I have a framed picture of our son, my brothers, and my mom on the log ride at SeaWorld in California. Those are memories that our son will never forget.

My kids have birthday party years. We always have a little family party, but every other year, we will have a friend party. If my spouse was going to be gone during a birthday party year, I might need to plan to have the party at a Chuck E. Cheese or a place that will allow everyone, *including me*, to enjoy a stress-free day. If you have been to a child's birthday party, you know how much work and planning it takes on the adult's part, so contracting it out will allow everyone to enjoy the day. It will be a new, special experience to remember.

The family may also experience a great deal of stress as they try to balance the demands of family life and the demands of preparing for the service member's departure. This can include planning for childcare, finding someone to take care of the household while the service member is away, and discussing wills and end-of-life decisions.

There are added steps when you live on base and use the base childcare. For example, my husband, an active-duty service member, had to sign a waiver and submit pay stubs to the childcare centers every year. The center would only take my signature if I had a special power of attorney permitting me to sign the paperwork required to continue using the services.

Acronyms are a big part of every organization, and the military is no different. The Child Development Center is also called the CDC, the Child Youth Programs for After-School Care are CYP, and the Teen Center is TCP. Base housing also requires that you submit pay stubs and signatures once a year.

I have a funny story about the acronyms. When I would refer to my daughter's daycare center as the CDC, which is what it is referred to on base, people who are not up on the acronyms would think that I had to go and pick my daughter up from the Centers for Disease Control. I seriously had coworkers ask a few times why my daughter was always at the Centers for Disease Control when I worked at places that were not military affiliated.

During this stage, preparation and communication are the theme. The more we prepare, the smoother things will be. When adults/kids/adolescents know what to expect, they feel secure and safe and have things to look forward to. This does not mean that everything in life must be predictable. Change happens, and it is a part of life, but trying to be prepared as best as possible makes the changes more bearable.

As the deployment gets closer, the command, unit, squadron, or whatever the group is called, is well into workups. It is evident that deployment is looming right around the corner. I go into frantic planning mode because there is a lot to consider. Some commands have their service members complete a pre-deployment and deployment checklist and are required to complete it before deployment. (I have added a checklist at the back in the appendix.)

The checklist covers topics such as putting legal affairs, such as banking, power of attorney, and wills, in order. Make sure passports and ID cards are up to date. If they are going to expire, make sure that the documentation for you is correct while deployed. These are emotionally charged, difficult conversations, and the list takes a good six weeks to complete. However, there are times when people learn about deployment with less time to prepare. In that case, the list is rushed, and alternate plans are put in place for the things that could not be completed.

It is also important to cover things like expectations you have during the deployment, such as the

> freedom to make independent decisions, contact with the opposite sex (fidelity), going out with friends, budgeting, child-rearing, and even how often letters or care packages will be sent. Failure to accurately communicate these and other expectations is frequently a source of misperception, distortion and hurt later in the deployment. (Pincus et al. 2007)

When my husband and I were stationed in Italy, we had to prepare a will. We had to discuss where our children would go if anything were to happen to us, and if anything happened, we had to discuss a plan or final wishes. It was a difficult topic to consider, but it needed to be done.

On the bright side, the legal affairs officer attached to his unit made the document official and ensured that we had other documents for free. If this service was provided in the community, a hefty fee would be required.

Don't let me overwhelm you, although it is an overwhelming time. If you feel like you need to stop and breathe, please do so. I need you to take care of yourself so you can take care of your family.

You cannot pour from an empty glass, take a break, and come back.

Remember, everything in life is a cycle. I have included many resources and an intensive deployment checklist in the appendix, covering just about everything for the spouse, children, and service member. Sometimes, the service member also gets a deployment checklist from the command, and an attorney usually deploys with commands so they can finish any loose ends.

During this stage, I will introduce you to dialectical behavior therapy, also called DBT. Please reflect on and familiarize yourself with the pages "What is DBT?" and "Wise Mind" and exercises in the appendix.

DBT is an approach by Marsha Linehan that acknowledges the possibility of two opposing beliefs being true simultaneously. To make the best decisions, we need to consider all the information available and weigh it against both our logical and emotional sides. This process is called Wise Mind, and it's illustrated in the appendix. We need to be mindful of both our rational and emotional sides to make the most informed decisions.

I utilize a variety of skills in my counseling practice. These include cognitive behavioral therapy (as practiced by Aaron Beck); the applied behavioral analysis of Ole Ivar Lovaas and B.F. Skinner; couples counseling (inspired by the Gottmans); attachment theory; Christian counseling; nurturing parenting (by Juliana Dellinger-Bavolek); and Thomas Phelan's *1-2-3 Magic*. If you are feeling stuck, seeking help from Fleet and Family or a counselor can be beneficial. Additionally, it's important to learn and adopt new skills to navigate difficult situations effectively. Turning to drugs, neglect, abuse, or alcohol is not an effective way to cope and can make the situation worse. Here is a short reminder list of useful skills in the appendix part of the book.

The pre-deployment checklist	DBT Distress Tolerance Exercises
Starfish Breathing	DBT Emotional Regulation Exercises
Mindfulness Exercises	Planning Exercises
The Speaker-Listener Technique	New Routines
Routines Worth Maintaining	

As you and your service member prepare for deployment, it's important to consider some of the difficult things you may encounter.

However, remember also to revisit the list of shared emotions. While being logical and reasonable during this process is important, attending to your feelings is equally important. If you don't, they may become overwhelming and create a significant emotional storm, making it difficult for you to focus on the tasks that need to be done.

Ready?

Okay, grab some tea, take a deep cleansing breath, sit back, and let's continue to discuss the anticipation of deployment but concentrate on our children, the kids in the household that the service member is deploying from.

Here is a list of common emotions/reactions in this stage.

- Sadness
- Irritability
- Anger
- Guilt
- Denial
- Anxiety
- Tension
- Frustration/restlessness
- Acceptance
- Loneliness
- Confusion
- Hopelessness
- Unpreparedness
- Stressed
- Headaches, stomachaches
- Trouble concentrating
- Loss of appetite
- Overeating
- Moodiness
- Trouble sleeping
- Excitement
- Resentment
- Numbness
- Emotional
- Displaced emotions
- Grief
- Stressed
- Freedom
- Excitement
- Trouble staying asleep
- Feeling like they are forgetting something
- Obsessive-compulsive symptoms over things like checking the door locks and making sure the oven is off (the symptoms experienced normally pertain to safety)
- Emotionally distancing themselves

My children had their reactions. The reactions experienced by different family members vary in range, intensity, frequency, reason, and display.

> Each child is born with about 23 billion brain cells. Brain cells are also called neurons. The neurons don't touch each other so when they communicate there is a communication highway called a synapse. A nerve impulse travels down the synapse to another nerve and the traveling creates an electrical impulse that stimulates the release of chemicals called neurotransmitters at the end other neuron. (Dellinger-Bavolek 2008)

Pre-schoolers may not understand what is going on, but they feel the tension. You might notice that they carry on as usual and react to the extra stress and emotions in the air, making them cling, whine, cry, or be more emotional and not know why. Printing out one of the emotional charts with pictures is an excellent activity to help children in this age group identify their feelings. There are a lot of valuable tools to help nonverbal, neurodivergent children identify or mirror how they feel, especially since the movie *Inside Out* was released.

Be patient and let them know that their feelings are normal. Read age-appropriate books about deployment, and talk about it calmly.

From my experience, some of the most common reactions from preschool children are being extra clingy, regressing significantly with toilet training, needing to be held, and needing to be comforted more than usual. Remember, they can anticipate a change. They don't understand what is happening. Change can be completely destabilizing for young children who thrive on routine and being able to predict what is next in their day.

School-age children can experience all the above reactions and feel confused because they don't understand why they are reacting the way they are. Remember when we talked about the brain and how it develops? Well, different parts of the brain develop at different times. The brain focuses on one area until it is fully developed, then focuses on another part. It is common for toddlers to dip in and out of negative feelings and become overly emotional. It is also likely that they will regress into old behaviors; sometimes that means bedwetting or suddenly needing a night light. I didn't mention bedwetting twice by accident.

Teenagers may feel pressure to make the most of the time they have left before the service member departs. The corporate factor may be a sense of obligation, guilt, shame, and negative thoughts. They could be filled with worry about the service member, their family, and how their lives are going to change. In addition to all the above reactions, they might withdraw more, experience unexpected tears over small things, spend more time with peers, challenge authority, act out, and act unbothered. They will try to keep their feelings in perspective by minimizing the changes. It is essential to communicate with children this age, have age-appropriate discussions, talk about the new routine, discuss what happens in case of an emergency, and who they can go to should there be an emergency. Provide them with space, acceptance, and assurance, and a healthy outlet or activity that is just for them.

There are a lot of elements to consider, such as trauma response, social and cognitive development, exceptionality, delayed development, or mental illness, and birth order.

Each child will have a different emotion, which will play out in his or her behaviors. If you reflect on the beginning of this section, I touched on how, in the beginning, children might not react too much to this stage. Cognitively, they might not have a concept of time or the ability to plan or make goals.

Common emotions from children

- Reacting to their parents' reactions
- Confusion
- Fear

- Sadness
- In their view, they are being abandoned, and it is a choice that their parents are making even if they cognitively know their parent has no choice. The feelings and emotions are real.
- Being upset
- Anger
- Anticipation of increased responsibility
- Short-temperedness
- Frustration
- Irritability
- Resentment
- Excitement as my son grew and experienced more frequent deployments. He began to look forward to them because we had a good routine. Our normal was having my spouse deployed. He knew what to expect, and routine expectations play a big role in making children feel safe and secure.
- Trouble sleeping
- Sleeping too much
- Bad dreams
- Bedwetting, accidents
- Overeating
- Undereating
- Loss of interest in activities they once enjoyed
- Clinginess
- Body aches
- Regression
- And all the emotions previously listed

Remember, routine and control help our children feel safe and secure. Deployment is a big event that they have no control over. Suggesting weekly family meetings as the deployment gets closer can help children, teenagers, or adolescents share their feelings and concerns, learn what they can expect about the parent's deployment, help make a plan for the house, and ensure things run smoothly.

For example, the child may help with laundry and fold socks while the parent is deployed. It might seem small and insignificant to us as adults, but for children, that is what they can do to help. Giving them routine, age-appropriate responsibilities and a chance to voice their opinions in a loving, safe, non-judgmental manner will help to foster safety, community, and independence within the family unit.

As the parent, it is important to keep in mind that all these emotions can present as intense anger, being overly emotional, and being short-tempered. The child will not understand his or her reaction or response, but the child's emotions are stronger than the child's logical ability at that time. As a result, the child acts out. When anticipating, disciplining, or experiencing intense behaviors from your children, stay mindful and be compassionate; they are struggling, too. If the reaction does not fit the situation, it could be due to a more significant issue. When emotions are high, things in our environments appear to snowball and can quickly become too much.

Losing a parent or caregiver due to deployment is a big deal.

While you are taking care of business and preparing for deployment in your way, your children are preparing and reacting to the emotions in their way. When all these intense emotions are not understood, it can result in extra tension, yelling, chaos, and a negative pre-deployment experience.

When my kids were young, they didn't understand, so the extra emotions that the adults were expressing were confusing for them. I remember that the children often reacted to our reactions.

In an EMDR training I attended, one of my favorite trauma instructors, Linda Curran, said emotions are transient, and it is true that emotions are contagious and pass from person to person.

Emotions are Transient (Linda Curran Trauma101.com)

We have talked about your reaction and your children's reaction, but what about your service members? They are still in the house at this point. Your service member will react too and more than likely feel the following.

- They may feel torn between their families and their units. Sometimes service members end up focusing more on the relationships between the people they are going to be deploying with than their families or spouses. Most of the time, this is not a conscious choice. The unit is hectically preparing for deployment, and there are last-minute training exercises, certifications, and equipment checks.
- They also need to bond with their units, comrades, and coworkers. They will need to depend on these people for a successful mission, and the goal is to make it back unharmed.
- Stress
- Regret
- Grief
- Relief
- Excitement
- Anger
- Detachment
- And all the emotions previously listed (Curran)

Deployment can be an incredibly stressful experience for both the service member and his or her family. Pre-deployment stressors can begin long before the separation as the service member and the family prepare for the upcoming deployment and the accompanying changes.

The service member and his or her family need to recognize that pre-deployment stress is every day and take steps to manage it. The service members should take care of their mental and physical health, and the families should seek support from friends and family or military support groups. The service member and his or her family can work together to manage pre-deployment stress and prepare for the upcoming deployment. The service member is also going to experience a range of feelings, such as fear, anxiety, worry, excitement to get it started and over with, guilt for leaving the family, worry, grief, and sorrow. They are more than likely trying to compartmentalize so they can do what they need to do.

Detachment and Withdrawal

Detachment and withdrawal are a normal part of the pre-deployment process. It is often more acceptable for people to leave if they withdraw or detach from the relationship because they are not experiencing the flood of emotions accompanying most separations. When people talk about this stage in the cycle, they often mention feeling detached, withdrawn, and uninterested, like they are dissociating, going through the movements, or empty.

Your service member may be preoccupied with the pre-deployment checklist, making sure that he or she is combat-ready, and it may feel like the person cares more about the command, unit, or operation than you. This is a normal feeling, and most of the time, it is not a realistic concern. Of course, the person still cares; the person is just doing what he or she needs to get by.

You, your service member, or both of you might have concerns about whether the relationship will survive the separation. Will my partner be faithful? What happens if he or she is hurt and is not the same as before? There are many worries and lists on either side of the relationship for the person maintaining the home front and the person deploying. It is important to maintain open communication and, being as understanding and non-judgmental as you can, establish a new way of communicating. A new way of communicating is that the service member may need to learn how often he or she can share or how he or she will be able to communicate via Skype, Facebook, email, phone, or snail mail. How often are you planning to send care packages? What will the service member want? I will add some tips and tricks on healthy communication in the appendix as well as different techniques for everyone to feel connected.

Often for me, the detachment and withdrawal phase looked like frustration. I would take responsibility for the kids and stop depending on my service member to do anything for me, the kids, or around the house. Remember, I said we needed to be honest and vulnerable. I would rather get used to doing everything (working my counseling schedule; dropping off and picking up the kids at school; disciplining; helping with schoolwork; going to sports or extracurricular activities, like ballet classes; cleaning; and taking out the trash) on my own because I knew I would not be able to depend on having his support and it would make it harder later. I would find myself fighting back the tears at random times during the day or while taking out the trash, doing the dishes, or taking a shower.

My girls were clingy and emotional and just wanted to be held by their dad. Our son tried to push my husband and me away. He wanted to hang out with his friends more or zone out listening to music while sitting on the swings at the park on base. Occasionally, I could see a tear fall from the side of his eye as he tried to ignore and push his emotions away.

Children, especially young children, will react two or three days before the departure as they notice the service member packing and putting the deployment bag by the door.

When our son was two years old, we were stationed in Virginia, and my husband was deployed. Our son would try to unpack my husband's bag or make room for himself, as little kids often do when someone is packing to leave. As the progression continued, he would try to take the bags away from the front door and back to the bedroom; of course, he couldn't. The bags were bigger than he was.

The drop-off was quick, but our son saw his dad's car in the apartment parking spot. Whenever we went for a walk or returned to the apartment, he got excited thinking Dad was home and insisted that Dad was playing hide and seek. We checked under every bed, in every room, and in every cabinet every time. We never played hide and seek as a family, but that is the explanation his little toddler two-year-old mind came up with. I had things planned to distract him, and we would typically see extended family when my husband deployed. That way, he could develop relationships with the family he rarely saw. It gave him a distraction and new experiences so he wasn't focused on Dad's car and hide and seek.

As deployment gets closer, the children in your life may be feeling

- sad;
- worried;
- anxious;
- emotionally detached;
- withdrawn;
- guilty;
- impatient;
- frustrated (especially if the deployment is delayed);
- responsible for the service member leaving (this is a hard one, but children really do think that the world revolves around them so in their mind it makes sense that they caused the service member to deploy or disappear); or
- ashamed,
- in addition to all the pre-deployment emotions previously listed.

Preschool children or children with developmental delays could express their feelings through tantrums, being clingy, mood swings, and fluctuating between being independent and significant dependence. They may have difficulty comprehending that a parent is leaving when the parent is still there.

School-aged children may experience tearfulness and sensitivity; they may express anger and not know why. They could be clingy and needy, wanting more physical contact and attention. Please make sure that you let the child's school and teacher know that he or she is experiencing these changes. That way, the teachers can be on the lookout for any changes. Also, be sure to check in with your children frequently. Remember that children are often impulsive, and the youngest child I worked with who attempted suicide was five years old. I have dozens of reports of second and third graders who want to go to sleep and not wake up or end the pain for various reasons.

You can expect teenagers to lash out, argue, be unwilling to talk about their worries, and try to push away or ignore their feelings. They will want to be out with friends. They would like information about the deployment or changes but want the information at different times. You should also expect changes in mood, eating, and sleeping patterns. Teenagers are school-aged children with bigger bodies. They are still impulsive, and because they don't require as much supervision, they have more opportunities to do things they are not emotionally or physically ready for. They are at a higher risk of partaking in mind-altering substances and behaviors that are or could be harmful. Keep communication open.

I developed a rule with my children once they were old enough to have cell phones or texting devices. I call it code X; I don't remember who created the rule. It was probably something I picked up on Facebook or a parenting website.

If one of the children texted me an X, I would know that child was in a situation he or she needed help getting out of. I would call the child and make up an emergency, explaining that I must pick him or her up immediately and then ask for the address. The caveat is that the child would not get in trouble because the child realized he or she was in a bad situation and asked for help.

I don't remember any behaviors with the pets during the anticipation stages. However, we had cats and dogs—normally two dogs and one cat.

When my husband was in the middle of workups, it was complicated because he was not home long enough to do anything "helpful" for the family. He would come home long enough to disrupt the new cycle that we as a family unit (the kids and I) had started, and then leave again. We would be overjoyed to see and hug him, but the kids and I had an excellent groove. We had a new morning routine, pick-up routines, and nighttime routines.

Change is difficult for everyone: adults, babies, pets, and especially toddlers. The first few days after your service member returns home and the first few days after he or she leaves for workups are adjustment days.

If you grew up in a blended family, remember how you felt on transfer days when you would return to your mom's house from your dad's. Then, you can relate a bit easier. The big difference is that these adjustments need to be more consistently implemented because the workup is leading up to the deployment. People excel with routines, so small breaks can be obnoxious. Have patience, love each other unconditionally, and know this too shall pass.

CHAPTER 5

Deployment

Deployment usually includes

3. emotional disorientation;
4. recovery and stabilization; and
5. anticipation of return.

We are at that most dreaded part of the cycle: the *deployment*. Right now, you should be driving back from dropping your service member off with his or her military bags. This is a confusing time because, on the one hand, you will likely feel like your heart is broken and you just went through the worst breakup you could imagine. You could be feeling abandoned and confused at the same time because, logically, you know it wasn't a breakup, and things will be fine. It is just a separation, and it has happened before.

The deployment process is an emotional journey for the entire military family. It can be stressful and challenging, but with the proper support and resources, it can also be a time of growth and transformation.

Deployment can bring a variety of emotional experiences, including excitement, anxiety, sadness, and uncertainty. It is essential to understand the emotional cycle of deployment and recognize its impact on military families.

When military members prepare to deploy, their family members may experience various emotions. They may feel proud of their loved one's service but also have feelings of fear and anxiety about what lies ahead. Communication is critical during this time and discussing feelings openly and honestly can be beneficial.

Once a military member is deployed, family members may feel lonely and isolated. They may also feel overwhelmed with responsibilities at home and have difficulty coping with the separation. It is essential to reach out and find support during this time. Various strategies are available to help family members cope with deployment separation, such as joining a support group, seeking counseling, and engaging in activities that bring joy.

We created a deployment tradition and would get ice cream every time after dropping off my husband, even for a workup.

Communication between my husband and me was more challenging. He was always on an aircraft carrier and the internet connection was not good. They could be in River City (that means all communication was down), or he didn't have time between his shifts. When the carrier pulled into a port, the internet connection, even if you paid for global cell service, was not great. A few of the people on the ship would get a hotel so they could have a good chunk of uninterrupted Facetime.

When the kids were little and he called, I would put the call on Bluetooth and run it over the speakers in my Dodge Caliber so the kids could hear his voice and talk to him, too. I would get the kids, run to the car, and sit in the car while in the driveway while we talked to Daddy. If I was driving when he called, I would pull over to the closest parking lot. We never knew when a call would come. If we missed it, we never knew, or it was hard to predict, when he could call again.

This brings me to advice or resource number one: create a secret language. Most of the time, they cannot give you dates or times, but sometimes they can through secret messages that only you would know. For example, suppose you will meet your spouse at a port in Australia, but you need to know the dates to buy plane tickets, rent a hotel, and so on. Your spouse might say something like, "I should be able to see you on the day our third child was born, in the month of Easter."

Our third child was born on the eighteenth, and Easter is either in March or April, depending on the year. That narrows down my information. Because deployments rarely go as planned, I know that he may or may not show up around that time, so I need to either have a refundable fare or plan on enjoying some alone time on my trip.

This is important because plans can change or be canceled on the drop of a dime and it is common that military things get rerouted, changed without notice.

Do not post anything that can be used to give information to others—no countdowns, no trip plans, not a thing. Tell your in-laws, parents, and significant others, *no posting* under any circumstances.

It is called OPSEC (Operations Security), another acronym and a way of life, but it is one of the more important ones you need to know and understand. What does that really mean?

The official Department of Defense definition is this.

> OPSEC thus is a systematic and proved process by which the U.S. Government and its supporting contractors can deny to potential adversaries information about capabilities and intentions by identifying, controlling, and protecting generally unclassified evidence of the planning and execution of sensitive Government activities. ("National Security Decision Directive Number 298")

Whoa! That's intense!

Did you get any of that? I know I am a little overwhelmed with that definition!

Nearly everyone can relate to this definition.

You can find free Wi-Fi just about anywhere. You never know who may be listening to your conversations, either in the cyber world or in person. This alone makes OPSEC one of the most important things you'll ever do to keep your service member and family safe.

Let's break it down and put it in terms you can understand. I will also tell you what you need to do to stay in OPSEC's good graces.

OPSEC is *not* a set of rules that tell you what to say or not. Instead, it is a process for denying adversaries access to critical information.

You want to ensure you are not providing our adversaries information that could harm our service members and military operations or change the military operation plan. In essence, it's a mindset you need to practice all the time and anywhere you are.

OPSEC indicators are those friendly actions and open sources of information that adversary intelligence systems can detect or obtain and then interpret to derive critical information.

Remember, adversaries frequently visit some of the same stores, clubs, recreational areas, places of worship, restaurants, and social networking sites as you do.

Maintaining situational awareness means staying safe and watching out for loved ones. Also, remember that following OPSEC is also good for your personal security (PERSEC) and your family because an adversary isn't always a terrorist. They could be thieves waiting for you to reveal when your house will be unoccupied or cyber-criminals wanting your information to steal your identity. I am not writing this to scare you but to keep you aware.

A few years ago, my husband was deployed overseas. Some girlfriends and spouses were excited to get a call and posted that I had just called X. Anyone reading that with ill intent could track, reverse track, and obtain coordinates. Then, another time, some spouses planned to visit their service members and texted and posted dates. Because of the seemingly innocent leak of information, the mission plans had to be changed. The deployment was extended, and scheduled breaks were canceled, meaning plans were altered, kids didn't get to see parents, and the spouse at home grieved all over again. The service member would be working harder and longer without a break, and sometimes, the limited communication would be cut off for months.

Please, take a minute and think about all the seemingly innocent information we share daily. Now, add all of the apps, phone towers, and webpages that ping and alert us to trouble, track our kids, and identify routines.

Emotional Disorientation

This stage begins right around deployment time. Written documentation says that it only lasts a few days. In my experience, this stage goes on until the recovery and stabilization stage starts, which they say is around the second month after deployment. You are reading this correctly. Intense emotions are expected, but during the emotional disorientation stage, you need to practice self-care and attempt to establish a new routine.

Emotional disorientation sounds scary, but if we break it down, it means emotional confusion. During this stage, is it common for everyone to feel these emotions.

Shock	Anxiety
Relief (the relief may be followed by a feeling of guilt because the person is relieved to get the deployment started)	Sense of anti–climax (exhaustion) Sense of disruption
Numbness	Confusion (this is especially true for children, who have a
Pain	limited understanding on what is happening)
Loneliness	Sense of being overwhelmed

It is common for preschoolers to regress to behaviors that they had finished, such as bedwetting, wanting to share a bed with their primary caregiver, or sucking their thumbs. Don't be surprised if you know of children who are diagnosed with autism, down syndrome, ADD, ADHD, and other neurodivergences to regress or display any of the reactions expected from different age categories. From my experience, regression is to be expected; this is a considerable change.

They may be extra clingy with people or a favorite toy or blanket.	Exhibiting sleep disturbances
	Exhibiting changes in eating patterns
They may display unexplained crying to tearfulness without understanding why they are crying.	Becoming fearful of new people or situations, or becoming emotional over small changes in daily plans
Hitting	Being more sensitive than usual
Biting people or things	

I have always been my children's person, the one who is always available no matter what, and who reinforces and teaches unconditional love. That meant I often experienced the good, the bad, and the ugly of our children's behaviors. Sometimes, it would be a struggle to remind myself that they were not yelling or saying mean things because they were mad at me. They were screaming, crying, and saying mean things because their emotional sides were overwhelmed. They knew they were safe and were going to be loved and accepted through it.

That does not mean that you are a doormat for your children; you expect to be treated with kindness and respect just as they are, and there are consequences for bad behavior. However, it means that you give your children the space to be emotional. After their tantrums, when they are rational again, talk about it, hug it out, and always tell them how proud you are of them. I call this a sandwich.

- Start with a positive.
- Talk about the thing that was not acceptable.
- End with a positive.

For example, when our son was young, he would cry and throw a tantrum for me but not his dad. As he got older and was in school, he occasionally showed me his good, bad, and ugly side. We would talk about it when he reset, used his skills, and calmed down.

As a mother going through it, you have to be mindful not to take their actions or words personally. Know that they are showing you that side because you make them feel safe, loved, and are teaching them what loving someone unconditionally looks like.

Looking back on our son and his outbursts when he was eight, nine, and ten years old, he experienced some displaced anger. We lived in California, and he attended counseling. Our son had some negative life experiences at the young age of seven and eight when we lived in Nevada. He did not understand what was happening to him emotionally or why his dad had to stay in Nevada while we moved to California. My husband and I were struggling, naturally. Our son thought that everything was his dad's fault and his dad was spiraling out of control because of everything that he experienced during his previous deployment and while living in Nevada. Our marriage and family counselor explained everything that was happening in our lives at that time as the perfect storm. As I look back, it really was. If I hadn't been in the middle of my master's degree, things might have ended very differently. My counseling program and my trauma response made it easy for me to dissociate and look at things from a different perspective. I knew deep down in every fiber of my being that I was a good wife and mother, and that sometimes, bad things happen to good people. What defines us as decent or good people is how we react to life's adversities. We have choices; we can learn, recover, and grow from the experiences or we can crumble and feel or be out of control.

Because of my past and my belief in God, I already understood that God can use a negative experience and reframe it into a beautiful learning experience. I understood that I don't need to know how or why things happen the way they do. I do believe that he uses those experiences to expand in his glory, to teach, and to positively impact the lives of others.

With our son's displaced anger, I also understood that because I was our son's stable person, the person who was going to give him and show him unconditional love, I was the person he felt safe enough to show his good, bad, and ugly to.

One day, when he was about eight, he was so mad, he punched the wall. He didn't do anything to the wall but hurt his hand. I didn't get angry. I didn't yell. I held him, consoled him, and acknowledged his pain. Afterward, we discussed how silly it was to hurt yourself and that punching the wall was an ineffective way of releasing emotions. I also signed him up for tae kwon do. This gave him a productive outlet for his emotional energy. I also acknowledged his small, good choices and decisions.

We also started a new tradition of cutting coupons for a specific, local frozen yogurt shop. Anytime he received a good grade on a test or made a good choice, we would have frozen yogurt, and he was able to pick the flavors and one topping.

School-aged children and teenagers may experience all of the signs listed above and the following.

An increase in complaints, such as stomachaches, headaches, or other illnesses

Drop in performance at school

Loss of interest in usual things and hobbies

Anger toward the parent at home, or sudden or unusual school problems

Getting into trouble at school, home, or outside.

Low self-esteem and self-criticism

Testing the limits to see if the if the rules are the same

Misdirected anger (disproportionate anger over small things directed toward their

support people (i.e., the parent who stayed and siblings)

The increase in complaints and headaches or migraines is valid. Granted, every deployment is stressful. My husband managed to be smack dab in the middle of every significant economic discrepancy from 1999 to 2019, which were all heavily publicized. School government and economic classes covered regular curriculum and current events. There were the threats from other countries. Movies that appealed to children had scenes of sinking aircraft carriers or fights on aircraft carriers. These were difficult for children whose parents were stationed on aircraft carriers.

You are probably wondering specifically what I am referencing. There are many examples of things that affected my family during deployments. They added to our son's feelings of stress, having headaches and somatic complaints, and needing time to rest. The movies that affected him the most were *Power Rangers* and *Transformers*. Both of these are great kids' movies, but we needed to be mindful of the scenes. Even though we knew Transformers are make-believe and, logically, he knew it was not the carrier his dad was on, emotionally, it felt as if these were true. For a child, that leads to a lot of confusion and bad dreams. Emotions are not controlled by logic or facts.

Emotions are not logical, which is why we need to be mindful and aware that our children may not have developed the awareness to separate emotions from logic. Emotions can also overpower a person's logical and rational sides, making things feel worse than they are or making things feel scary that aren't. Sometimes, it has to do with an image that brings on an emotional response. What the image is associated with can provides us with information in the range of emotions and behaviors.

My daughter and son needed extra self-care during these times; they required more mom time and time to rest and just be. My advice for parents of children this age would be to listen to your children. Watch their behaviors, and remember that many of the kids who are emotionally suffering may not show any signs until it is too late. Kids are impulsive by nature; talk to them and give them a plan so that they know what to do if they feel a specific way. We teach about scenarios when predators come into the picture, if a stranger asks them if they need a ride, how to say no to drugs, and what to do in case of a fire or school shooter. We should also talk about what to do when they are feeling depressed or like they want to hurt themselves. Remember, the youngest child I worked with who tried to commit suicide was five years old and in kindergarten. I have worked with about a handful of children between six and eight years old who have written notes about wanting to die and not exist. Those children are in second and third grade!

I know it is hard to sometimes put down our electronic devices, especially because we never know when to anticipate a call from our deployed loved ones, but we must really try. Keep the volume on your phone up and close by but give your kids and family who are present your undivided attention. It matters a lot.

Recovery and Stabilization

A feeling of calm, increased confidence, and having adjusted to the new routine characterize this stage. You know what to expect, your kids know what to expect, and you may even find days when you are surviving and thriving. According to Jennifer Hochlan, "During this time, you will discover your independence, your abilities, and your enduring strength" (Hochlan 2017).

Many rely on the Family Readiness Group (FRG), a close network that meets on a regular basis to handle problems and disseminate the latest information. Others are more comfortable with family, friends, church, or other groups as their main means of emotional support. As challenges come up, most spouses learn that they are able to cope with crises and make important decisions on their own. They report feeling more confident and in control. During the sustainment stage, it is common to hear military spouses say, "I can do this!"

Given the speed and ease of information, discussing "hot topics" in a marriage can be problematic and are probably best left on hold until after the deployment when they can be resolved more fully. Obvious exceptions to this rule include a family emergency (i.e., the critical illness of a loved one) or a joyful event (i.e., the birth of a child). In these situations, the ideal route of communication is through the Red Cross so that the soldier's command is able to coordinate emergency leave if required (Pincus et al. 2007)

Anticipation of Return

During this stage, the family anticipates their service member's homecoming. This stage starts about a month before the deployed service member is due home. The family will be excited and happy and may have a boost in energy. This stage has been described as the "nesting period." It is common for people to have trouble making decisions while they are preparing for the military member to return home.

Some concerns the spouse could be preoccupied with include wondering if the service member will agree with the changes the spouse made, if the spouse will have to give up his or her independence, or whether the two will get along. Ironically, even though the separation is almost over, there can be renewed difficulty in making decisions. This is due, in part, to increased attention to choices that the returning member might make.

A complete "to-do" list often exists before their mates return, especially around the home. It is almost inevitable that expectations will be high.

The other reactions are similar to the pre-deployment and deployment stages because everyone in the house anticipates and remembers change is hard. Generally, people don't prefer change because fear of the unknown typically accompanies it.

Some extra tips that I have for new spouses in this stage are not planning a homecoming party and not planning to go anywhere populated like Disneyland. I learned the Disneyland one by making that mistake myself.

In the summer of 2011, my husband was returning from a deployment. I had an almost one-year-old and a five-year-old. The plan was that after our four-day Disneyland trip, we were moving (transferring) to a new base and into base housing. I was so excited. I had hotel reservations at the Grand California Hotel the kids were going to love. The hotel was close enough that if anyone needed a nap, the person could return to the hotel. I saved and paid for it, and in my mind, everything was great.

Well, my husband was coming off a rather negative deployment; he lost a good friend to suicide. My husband was having dreams of the interactions he had with this friend the day before he successfully committed suicide. My husband worked the night shift the entire deployment and was stressed about money, crowds, and responsibility. He struggled and tried to hide most of it. We argued a lot about money, mainly how much the trip cost, how long the lines were, and what I was or wasn't doing that he thought I should be.

We checked out on day two, received refunds for the two other days, returned home, and moved to Fallon, Nevada.

Physical intimacy is also not what most spouses fantasize that it will be. When I worked at the Fleet and Family, I would give classes (briefs) to spouses of the returning commands. I informed them that the first time they were intimate with their spouses, it would probably not be romantic. It would be sneaky and quick—wham, bam, thank you, ma'am. However, it can be fun in the coat closet or on top of the washing machine. This first time will be more like a wild animalistic type of meeting the need so that you can focus on love and reconnecting later.

CHAPTER 6

Post Deployment

Return, Adjust, Reintegrate

When a military member returns home, the family may experience various emotions. Reuniting after a deployment is a time of joy but also a time of adjustment. Understanding the emotional reunion after deployment and how to transition back into post-deployment life is essential.

Deployment can also have an effect on intimate relationships, including marriages and partnerships. It is important to recognize the impact of deployment on intimate relationships and to develop communication strategies to ensure a successful transition back into family life.

The deployed spouse and the at-home spouse are together physically but not necessarily emotionally. They will have to spend time together and share experiences and feelings before they feel like a couple again. They both need to be aware of the necessity to refocus on the marriage.

> For instance, After one of the wives' husbands had been home for a few days, she became aggravated when he would telephone his shipboard roommate every time something of importance came up within the family, declaring, "I'm your wife. Talk to *me!*" Too much togetherness initially can cause

friction after so many months of living apart. (Logan 2021)

As far as communication between spouses goes, assumptions will not work. Some find that "talking as we go along" works best. I have added in the appendix a speaker-listener technique that will help break things down and make sure that each person is heard. I have had a lot of luck with this technique. The couples that I have counseled who started following the technique had better results than the couples who tried freestyle dialogue.

Logan also states, "Sexual relations, ardently desired before the return, may initially seem frightening. Couples need sufficient time together to become reacquainted bee fore they can expect true intimacy" (Logan 2021).

This stage can be difficult as well as joyful. Nevertheless, it does provide an opportunity offered to few civilian couples: the chance to evaluate what changes have occurred within themselves, to determine what direction they want their growth to take, and to meld all this into a renewed and refreshed relationship.

Finally, it is important to recognize the long-term effects of deployment on mental health. It can be beneficial to seek counseling and other forms of support to ensure that the entire family can adjust to post-deployment life.

The deployment process is an emotional journey for the entire military family. It is essential to be aware of the emotional cycle of deployment, the impact of deployment on military families, and the strategies available to cope with deployment separation. Additionally, understanding the emotional reunion after deployment, adjusting to post-deployment life, and recognizing the impact of deployment on intimate relationships is essential. Finally, it is crucial to be aware of the long-term effects of deployment on mental health and to develop communication strategies during deployment.

Reintegration and Stabilization

The second stage is the actual reunion. This is a time of reconnecting and reestablishing the family dynamic. It is important to understand that the reunion process can be challenging, and there can be feelings of awkwardness, anxiety, and even disappointment. It is important to be patient and understanding during this time.

Next, the family members adjust to life together and reestablish routines and relationships. It is essential to address any issues that may have arisen during deployment, such as changes in parenting styles or communication difficulties. It is also necessary to take the time to enjoy being together.

The reunion process can be a challenging but ultimately rewarding experience. It is important to allow time for family members to adjust to the idea of reuniting and to prepare for the transition. It is also important to be patient and understanding during the reunion and to take the time to enjoy being together. Additionally, addressing any issues that may have arisen during deployment is important to ensure a successful transition back into post-deployment life.

Rinse and repeat.

As Logan states, "Once this or cycle is understood, we can examine the effects of other kinds of deployments. It takes time to work through each stage; people's emotions cannot be forced to fit ships' schedules" (Logan 2021).

Many problems in families experiencing deployment could be avoided or minimized simply by understanding the process of adjustment. For example, lack of sexual intimacy just before deployment could be accepted as a natural reaction to difficult circumstances rather than being viewed as personal rejection.

Arguing during that time may be tolerated instead of perceived as evidence of a deteriorating marriage. It also helps to know that it is perfectly normal to feel somewhat strange with each other when the deployed spouse first comes home. Almost everyone feels reassured just knowing that his or her range and fluctuation of emotions is normal (Logan 2021).

Deployment Resources

1. Policy and oversight information and guidance from the Defense Health Agency, Public Health Division, Deployment Health Branch can be found at https://info.health.mil/hco/phealth/deployment_health/.
2. DeploymentHealthProductLine/Forms/Allitems.aspx (CAC required)
3. Military and Family Life Counseling (MFLC): Counseling is available to address improving relationships at home and work, stress management, adjustment difficulties, parenting, and grief or loss. They are also available at elementary schools and preschools on military bases.
4. Military chaplains: Consulting with your chaplain is strictly confidential. The chaplain is available on base and detached to each command.
5. The Military Base Guide is available at https://www.military.com/base-guide.
6. For information about $4,000 scholarships for military spouses, visit https://mycaa.medcertify.com/mycaa-bing/?msclkid=1191c71905bc19758118a2cbe8f8f54b.
7. Armed Forces Vacation Club: https://www.afvclub.com/account/login?utm_campaign=NonBrand_Evergreen_OpenMarket_AFVC_FY24&utm_source=bing&utm_medium=paid-search_conversion&utm_content=text_militaryhotels&msclkid=9fb9150d34911087178670dfd93bd9b3
8. *Sesame Street* Workshop for Deployed Service Members: https://sesameworkshop.org/our-work/impact-areas/military-families/

9. *Sesame Street* programing for military families: https://www.militaryonesource.mil/resources/millife-guides/sesame-street-resources/

10. Daddy Dolls: https://hugahero.com/

11. Request free care packs for your troop at https://www.troopathon.org/request-a-military-care-package.

12. Read "Sending a Military Care Package: What You Need to Know" on https://www.militaryonesource.mil/relationships/support-community/sending-a-military-care-package/.

13. Free tutoring for kids is available at https://military.tutor.com/home.

14. The Military Wife and Mom website has great information and resources: https://themilitarywifeandmom.com/

15. Individual Mobilization Augmentee (IMA) Program, Army Human Resources Command (HRC) (requires Common Access Card (CAC) login)

16. Army Reserve Individual Ready Reserve (IRR), IMA, United States Army Reserve Command (USARC) Augmentation Unit (UAU), and IA

17. IMA Program, Marine Corps Mobilization Command (MobCom)

18. United States Navy IA Sailor, Family, Command, and Employer, United States Fleet Forces Command

19. Expeditionary Combat Readiness Center (ECRC), Navy Expeditionary Combat Command

20. Air Force Reserve Command (AFRC)

21. Military.com and Military OneSource.mil: https://www.militaryonesource.mil/

22. https://www.military.com/base-guide is a military base directory.

APPENDIX

What is dialectical behavior therapy? In 1980, Marsha Linehan and her team wanted to create a more effective way to treat suicidal behavior and borderline personality disorder (BPD). Fast forward to 2024, and DBT is adequate for most people. DBT is a skills-based therapy. We can all use skills in mindfulness, distress tolerance, interpersonal effectiveness, and emotional regulation. I will add a few of the DBT skills that I have adapted for military families and that are helpful to most in just about any situation. You need to see a therapist certified in DBT, attend skill groups, and learn the skills in a structured way that will promote your growth and understanding in order to utilize the full program and all the skills. I am attaching a few mindful, distress tolerance, and interpersonal effectiveness skills that I have adapted from other DBT therapists to fit the military lifestyle.

> DBT is a form of CBT. Palmer refers to it as a "Strange hybrid" of a number of different therapies and techniques...I usually respond that, in terms of skills DBT is CBT using a different language, with the addition of mindfulness and acceptance techniques. DBT takes the judgment out of CBT. (Van Dijk 2012, page)

> DBT is principal driven where CBT tends to be protocol driven. (Swales and Heard 2009, page)

One of the central tenets of DBT is the wise mind. Wise mind is the "blend of emotional mind and reason mind" (Rathus and Miller 2015, page). Emotions are not logical and don't always fit the situation; sometimes, people tend to be impulsive, to overreact or not react, or appear to be stuck in a functional freeze, especially during stressful events like deployments. The distress tolerance skills should be helpful in distracting your mind and resetting your nervous system so you can reevaluate and make informed decisions.

You must also consider if your body is in fight or flight. If your reaction does not fit the scene, you feel defensive, judged, and emotional, you are likely operating out of a fight or flight response. I also describe this stage as "kill or be killed." The logical part of the brain, also known as the cerebral cortex and prefrontal cortex, is responsible for executive functioning, making sense of the world, and other advanced functions like reasoning to keep you safe. Dr. Dan Sigel does a fantastic job of explaining this in the hand model of the brain. I will link his information in the helpful resources section and some tremendous books I recommend to most of my friends and clients. In the hand model, the amygdala is one of the parts responsible for igniting the fight or flight response. It is now called the fight, flight, freeze, or faint response. Remember, those can be big responses because the person is in a kill-or-be-killed mode. When you are making a decision or in an argument with a person and you notice that this reaction is happening, a helpful idea would be to take a break, use a distress tolerance technique, and let your body return to a calm state before returning to the discussion. I will also have a DBT interpersonal effectiveness skill called "Dear Man" and a technique I call the speaker-listener technique to help you in some of these difficult interactions. You should still seek help from a professional therapist to learn more. We should all seek therapy at some point to help us understand things differently. These are my first go-to skills, which you have probably been doing your entire life; the difference is that now you are doing them mindfully, which is so empowering.

THE SPOUSES' DEPLOYMENT CHECKLIST

Keeping your family on track and organized for a successful deployment.

- Practical Preparation
- Vehicles
- Financial Preparation
- Preparation for Emergency
- Plans for Housing
- Service Member Personal Preparation
- Non-Deploying Spouse
- Extra Helpful Information
- Emergency Numbers/Support Websites

Practical Preparation

- ❑ Ensure dependent ID cards are up to date and are not supposed to expire while the service member is deployed. (Deers Verification 1-800-538-9952)
- ❑ Update driver's license and passports.
- ❑ Update Emergency Data Form or Page 2.
- ❑ Update family contact information in the Navy Family Accountability and Assessment System (NFAAS) under practical preparation or emergency prep.
- ❑ File power of attorney.
- ❑ Make a valid will.
- ❑ Updated Servicemembers Group Life Insurance (SGLI) with the correct beneficiary information.
- ❑ Make sure the family knows the complete official mailing address, the command name, the service member's rank and rate, and the sponsor's social security number.

- ❑ Make sure the family has command contact information, including Family Readiness Group (FRG) and ombudsman information.
- ❑ Make sure renter's or homeowner's insurance is current and that the home or apartment is in good repair.

Vehicles

- ❑ If necessary, store the vehicle or arrange for someone to take care of it.
- ❑ Make sure insurance, tags, registration, title, and base inspection stickers are all current, and routine maintenance has been performed.
- ❑ Provide the name of trusted mechanic/repair garage if the vehicle is left with family.
- ❑ Have someone run it once every few weeks, unplug the battery, and prepare vehicles for long-term storage.
- ❑ Call the insurance company and let them know the car will be stored while you are in deployment; it will save on insurance.

Financial Preparation

- ❑ Create a monthly spending plan for the deployment, including any pay changes and additional deployment-related expenses. (Pay always changes. It decreases the first month and balances out the second. Sometimes, there is even extra combat or sea pay and tax-free zones included.)
- ❑ If married, discuss a budget, and make sure your spouse knows when paydays are.
- ❑ Make arrangements to pay bills, including to creditors. (If you call the credit card companies and let them know you will be deployed, many of them will stop the interest while you are deployed).

- ❏ Make sure allotments or online banking is set up. (If you have a family, an allotment should be set for household expenses and a separate allotment or account for deployment-related expenses.)
- ❏ Set up a cell phone with a long-distance or out-of-country plan.
- ❏ Make sure that, once a year, expenses such as taxes or insurance are covered.
- ❏ Are taxes due while deployed? Plan for payment or extension.
- ❏ Know credit card limits and, if married, who will be using which cards.
- ❏ Know about emergency funds, savings plan, or savings deposit programs, if eligible. Investigate Thrift Savings Plans (TSP).

Preparation for Emergency

- ❏ Know the location of emergency paperwork, such as birth certificates, Social Security cards, immunization records for people and pets, marriage license, and power of attorney paperwork.
- ❏ Does your spouse know how to assess the TRICARE system for medical care when outside the local area? Do you need to consider signing a preauthorization form with the Navy-Marine Corps Relief Society?
- ❏ Have an evacuation plan. If there is an evacuation, who do you call for information about your family?

Plans for Housing

- ❏ If you are planning to sublet your house or apartment, did you do a credit check for potential clients?
- ❏ If subletting your house or apartment, do you have a property manager who is authorized to make repairs and check on the property?

- [ ] Is your renter's or homeowner's insurance current, and does it cover repairs or replacement costs?
- [ ] Do you have a plan for routine maintenance and yard care?

Service Member Personal Preparation

- [ ] Do you have uniforms, civilian clothes, and personal items for use while deployed?
- [ ] Do you have phone numbers, addresses, and email addresses of family and friends?
- [ ] Have you made arrangements for birthdays and special occasions?
- [ ] Have you discussed "keeping in touch" with friends and family?
- [ ] Have you made plans for education and courses already underway?
- [ ] Is the Family Care Plan in order?

Non-Deploying Spouse

- [ ] Do you have the deploying spouse's banking, Netflix, Disney Plus, and other subscription passwords?
- [ ] Make sure your name is on the accounts as an authorized user and set the recovery e-mail to an e-mail account or phone number you have access to.
- [ ] Do you have power of attorney authorizing you to make decisions on the children's behalf? (If you plan to use the Child Development Center (CDC) or the Child and Youth Programs (CYP) on base at all, you need this power of attorney. It is a specific one and may be called something different depending on your branch, but the service member or FRG will know.)
- [ ] Discuss a private code to use when communicating with your spouse; an example could be, "I will call you on our first

child's birthday." You will not need to speak in code all the time, but when you need to, you will understand.

☐ Make sure you are connected online with the command, squadron, and base. Much Family Readiness Group (FRG) information is sent over the internet.

☐ Be aware of Operational Security (OPSEC) and know what is public knowledge and what is not. Loose lips sink ships. Use caution when posting or talking about future plans, celebrations, trips, calls, and dates.

☐ Be aware of what your children know. Plans are often canceled or changed at the last minute, and children often don't have a filter, especially when they are excited because they are anticipating a reunion.

Extra Helpful Information

☐ Many young families will terminate their leases and move to a family member's home when the service member is deployed. You can legally terminate your housing or car lease under the Servicemembers Civil Relief Act.

☐ For legal documents, such as a power of attorney and will, you do not need to pay a fee out of town. The installation legal services office can update legal information and draft specific documents.

Emergency Numbers/Support Websites

☐ FRG—Fleet and Family Support Center Command Information
☐ Address to send care packages to
☐ Home warranty phone number
☐ Doctors' numbers
   o Yours
   o Children's
   o Dentist

- o Urgent Care
- o Pharmacy
- o Therapy providers (speech, occupational therapy, clinical counseling)
- ❑ Veterinary Clinic
  - o Urgent Care Vet
- MilitaryOneSource: https://www.militaryonesource.mil
- *Sesame Street* for military children: https://sesamestreetformilitaryfamilies.org
- Free 24/7 online tutoring and homework help: https://military.tutor.com/home

The National Suicide Prevention Lifeline is now the 988 Suicide and Crisis Lifeline.

Poison Control: https://www.poison.org/. Contact Poison Control right away if you suspect a poisoning. Help is available online or by phone at 1-800-222-1222. Both options are free, expert, and confidential.

Appendix Table of Contents

- What is Mindfulness?
- Tips to Begin a Mindfulness Practice
- Benefits of a Mindfulness Practice
- Mindful Walk
- Mindful Walk Graphic
- Mindful Gratitude
- Breathing Techniques
- Starfish Breathing
- Starfish Breathing Graphic
- Breathing with Bubbles
- Deep Breathing with Prompts
- Encouraging Other People to Breathe
- DBT Wise Mind

- Wise Mind Accepts
- DBT Distress Tolerance
- Why Bother Tolerating Painful Urges?
- TIPP
- Weekly Habit Tracker
- DBT Interpersonal Effectiveness
- DEAR MAN
- Dr. Dan Siegel, Hand Model of the Brain and Why You Need to Understand the Reactions to Have Healthy Communication
- Speaker-Listener Technique

WHAT IS MINDFULNESS?

•• Intentionally living with awareness in the present moment

Waking up from automatic behaviors to participate and be present in our lives

•• Without judging or rejecting the moment, noticing consequences, discerning helpful and harmful behaviors while letting go of evaluating, avoiding, suppressing, or blocking the present moment

•• Mindfulness is taking control of your thoughts instead of letting your thoughts lead you.

•• Mindfulness can be practiced anytime, anywhere while doing anything. Intentionally pay attention to the moment without judgment.

TIPS TO BEGIN A MINDFULNESS PRACTICE

1. Approaching situations with a learner's mind

    Being curious and looking at things as new and interesting

2. Being non-judgmental; not labeling things as good or bad

    (It is what it is.)

3. Acknowledge the moment and acknowledge the feelings.

    Acknowledgment is not an agreement. It means "I hear and I see your experience."

4. Intentionally living with awareness in the present moment means less time with automatic behaviors, like zoning out.

Tips to Begin a Mindfulness Practice

Being mindful requires that we utilize eight attitudes most of the time.

1. Learner's Mind: Seeing everything as new and interesting
2. Non-judgmental: Avoiding labels of right or wrong, good or bad
3. Acknowledgment: Recognizing things as they are
4. Settled: Being grounded and comfortable in the moment
5. Composed: Remaining patient and in control
6. Letting Be: Letting things be with no need to change them
7. Self-Reliant: Deciding on your own, from your own experiences, what is true or not
8. Self-Compassionate: Loving yourself, your thoughts, and emotions as they are

Benefits of a Mindfulness Practice

Spending ten minutes a day being mindful can

- reduce suffering and increase happiness;
- increase control of your thoughts instead of letting your thoughts control you;
- allow you to experience reality as it is;
- increase your serotonin, dopamine, and oxytocin neurotransmitters (the happy hormone mix) naturally;
- lower your cortisol (stress hormone) levels;
- increase your overall health, leading to increased resilience and less sick time; and
- improve memory, improve emotional regulation, and increase behavioral control.

MINDFUL PRACTICE

MINDFUL SENSES WALK

Take a walk and bring your attention to

- five things you can see;
- four things you can feel;
- three things you can hear;
- two things you can smell; and
- one thing you can taste.

See, Touch, Hear, Smell, Taste

Mindful
Gratitude

Take a moment to examine your
strengths, your beliefs, and your
values; list all the attributes you are
proud of about you.

You are EXCEPTIONAL, one of a kind.
There has never been and never will
be another you!
Spending time to reflect on the
positive parts of you increases the
positive brain connections.

_____
_____
_____
_____
_____
_____
_____

Breathing Techniques

The Benefits of Mindful Breathing

- Release endorphins from the brain to promote a sense of relaxation by decreasing anxiety.

- Relieve stress from the body, which will decrease fatigue.

- Release muscle tension and decrease pain.

- Help your brain and body get oxygen, increasing your ability to be in a wise mind, think rationally, and respond appropriately.

> "When breathing, on the inhale, you nourish your mind and body, and on the exhale, you release stress and toxins.
> It can help to calm our nervous system and bring overall balance to our bodies. Breathwork is so powerful because it can be used as a tool to completely shift your energy." ~
> Sughesti, F. 2009. The power of Breathwork.

Starfish Breathing

1. Trace the outside of your hand with the pointer finger from your other hand.
2. As you trace your thumb up breathe in for 5 seconds.
3. At the top of your thumb, hold for 5 seconds.
4. Follow the arrows breathing out, tracing down the side of your thumb for 5 seconds.
5. Repeat this pattern in for 5, Hold for 5, Out for 5 Hold for 5 until you have traced all your fingers.

Breathing
With Bubbles

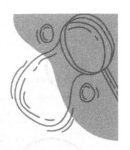

Blowing Bubbles is a great way to slow down and breathe. Breathe through your nose, expand your belly, then slowly breathe out. You have to have control of your breath to make the bubbles float without popping them.

Adapted from the Coping Skills for Kids workbook, by Halloran, 2018

Deep Breathing with Prompts

For some people having a prompt is helpful when trying to breathe deeply. There are many techniques, such as the following.

1. Ask questions that inspire the other person to take a deep breath. Take a deep, exaggerated breath and ask, "Do you smell that?" Pause and take another breath, then ask if the person smells _____ (a pleasurable memory). For kids, asking if they smell chocolate chip cookies and talking about baking cookies is enough to redirect their attention to breathing, allowing you to transition to another subject. For adults, ask if they smell gas or something that will encourage them to look for the phantom smell.
2. Breathe in like you are smelling a flower and breathe out like you are blowing out a birthday candle.
3. Breathe in, arms up; breathe out, arms down.
4. Breathe in a blue sky; breathe out gray skies.
5. Breathe in like Darth Vader.
6. Pretend your belly is a balloon. Breathe in and make the balloon bigger, then slowly breathe out, making the balloon shrink.[1]

Tips to Encourage Other People to Breathe

When you notice that someone needs to take deep, slow breaths and know that telling them to breathe or calm down will not go well, you can try the following.

*   Walk into the room and act like you smell something that will bring up a good memory or get the person to be a detective,

---

[1] Adapted from the *Coping Skills for Kids Workbook* by Janine Halloran (2018) and *DBT Skills Manual for Adolescents* by Jill Rathus and Alec Miller (2015).

like finding a gas leak. It will look like this. You walk into the room and take a deep, exaggerated sniff. Let the other person wait a few seconds and then ask if he or she smells anything. Curiosity will get the best of the person, and he or she will become distracted by trying to uncover the mystery smell.

- Take another two or three deep sniffs through the nose and out the mouth, then suggest a smell like cookies. Suggesting smells that have good memories associated with them will give your brain a dose of dopamine, oxytocin, serotonin, and endorphins, the chemicals released when someone feels loved, calm, energized, and happy.

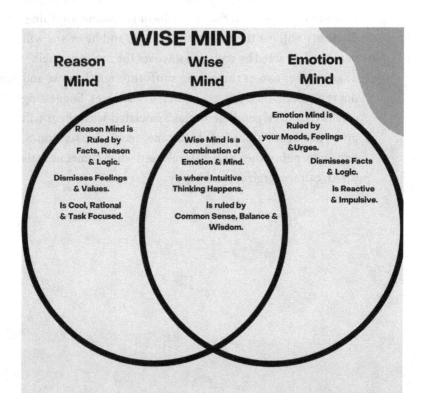

WISE MIND

Reason Mind **Wise Mind** **Emotion Mind**

Reason Mind is Ruled by Facts, Reason & Logic.

Dismisses Feelings & Values.

Is Cool, Rational & Task Focused.

Wise Mind is a combination of Emotion & Mind.

is where Intuitive Thinking Happens.

is ruled by Common Sense, Balance & Wisdom.

Emotion Mind is Ruled by your Moods, Feelings &Urges.

Dismisses Facts & Logic.

Is Reactive & Impulsive.

We all have three states of mind.
Reason Mind is driven by facts and figures.
Emotion Mind is driven by our emotions.
Wise Mind is a blend of a reason mind & emotion
mind. It is the wisdom within to avoid acting
impulsively.

Skill adapted from DBT Skills Training Handouts and Worksheets, Second Edition by Marsha M. Linehan, 2015

WISE MIND ACCEPTS

In the moment, distressing emotions may seem impossible to overcome. In time, these emotions will lessen in intensity and eventually fade away. The acronym ACCEPTS outlines seven techniques for distracting yourself from distressing emotions until they pass.

Activities: Do an activity that requires thought and concentration. • Read a book. • Write in a journal. • Do a project. • Play a sport. Watch a movie.

Contributing: Do something that allows you to focus on another person. • Ask a friend about his or her day. • Make a gift for a loved one. • Volunteer. • Send a thoughtful card.

Comparisons: Put your situation in perspective by comparing it to something more painful or distressing. • Think of a time when you were more distressed and realize how things are not as bad right now. • Realize your resilience by thinking of someone coping less well than you.

Emotions: Do something to create a new emotion that will compete with your distressing emotion. • Sad? Watch a happy movie. • Anxious? Practice deep breathing. • Angry? Go for a walk.

Pushing away: Avoid a painful situation or block it from your mind using a technique such as imagery. • Try to delay harmful urges for one hour. If the urge doesn't pass, put it off for another hour. • Imagine putting your negative thoughts in a box, taping it shut, and putting it in the back of your closet.

Thoughts: Use a mental strategy or an activity to shift your thoughts to something neutral. • Starting with the letter A, name objects around you that start with each letter of the alphabet. • Count a specific object around you. • Sing a song out loud or recite it in your head.

Sensations: Find safe physical sensations to distract you from distressing emotions. Hold an ice cube in your hand. • Eat something sour or spicy. • Take a cold shower.[2]

---

[2] Skill adapted from *DBT Skills Training Handouts and Worksheets*, 2nd ed., by Marsha M. Linehan (2015).

ACCEPTS

On a piece of paper or in a journal, respond to the following prompts to create your own ACCEPTS plan for tolerating distress.

Activities: List activities requiring concentration that would distract from your distressing emotion.

Contributing: List activities that allow you to focus on others instead of your distressing emotions.

Comparisons: Describe a time when you struggled with your distressing emotion but showed resilience. Recall this experience when faced with the emotion again.

Emotions: How can you create a new emotion that competes with your distressing emotion?

Pushing away: How can you avoid thoughts and situations that create distressing emotions?

Thoughts: List mental strategies or activities that would distract you from your distressing emotion.

Sensations: How can you create a safe physical sensation to distract from your distressing emotion?[3]

---

[3] Skill adapted from *DBT Skills Training Handouts and Worksheets*, 2nd ed., by Marsha M. Linehan (2015).

DISTRESS TOLERANCE SKILLS

Distress tolerance skills help people tolerate difficult situations and emotional pain when problems cannot be solved right away.

If you don't deal with or face the pain, you may act impulsively.

Ignoring the pain only increases the suffering.

When people act impulsively, they are more likely to make harmful decisions.

WHY BOTHER WITH PAINFUL URGES?

Sometimes, pain can't be avoided.

If you don't recognize your pain, you may act impulsively.

You may hurt yourself or someone you care about when you act impulsively.

The struggle can build resiliency and confidence.[4]

TIPP

Temperature, Intense Exercise, Paced Breathing, Progressive Muscle Relaxation

Temperature: Change your body temperature by splashing cold water on your face. Hold your breath, put your face in a bowl of cold water (above 50 degrees Fahrenheit). Hold a cold pack, frozen eye mask, or

---

[4] Skill adapted from *DBT Skills Manual for Adolescents* by Jill Rathus and Alec Miller (2015).

zip lock bag with ice or ice water on your eyes, cheeks, or the back of your neck and hold it for thirty seconds. Take a shower and stand in the water. Drink a cold drink.

Disclaimer: Ice water decreases your heart rate rapidly. Intense exercise will increase your heart rate. If you have a heart medical condition, lowered base heart rate due to medications, take a beta blocker, or have an eating disorder, consult your health care provider before using these skills. Avoid ice water if allergic to cold.

TIPP skills help to tip your body chemistry rapidly. These skills can be used when you are not thinking clearly. TIPP also builds on the natural, happy emotional transmitters.

TIPP YOUR BODY CHEMISTRY WITH
temperature, intense exercise, paced breathing, and progressive muscle relaxation.

Temperature: Changing your body temperature changes your body chemistry and helps to reset your nervous system. You can splash cold water on your face, or rub an ice cube in your hands, on the back of your neck, and on your forehead. Wear a cold gel eye mask. Drink a cold drink or suck on an ice cube.

Intense Exercise: Engaging in intense aerobic exercise, even for a short time, will expend stored-up energy and give you a dose of the happy hormones you get from working out.

Paced Breathing: Slowing your breathing down can help bring down arousal and allow more oxygen to get to the frontal cortex, helping to regulate the mind and body. Try the starfish breathing technique or breathe in to the count of five and out to the count of seven, making the exhale longer than the inhale.

Progressive Muscle Relaxation: Tense and relax each muscle group, head to toe, one muscle group at a time. Tense for five seconds, then let go, and relax each muscle all the way through. Notice the feelings of tension and the letdown.[5]

---

[5] Skill adapted from *DBT Skills Manual for Adolescents* by Jill Rathus and Alec Miller (2015).

WEEKLY HABIT TRACKER

DATES:

NOTES:

MORNING & DAYTIME ROUTINE

M T W T F

The hand model of the brain

Daniel J. Siegel, *Mindsight* (Melbourne: Scribe, 2010), p.15

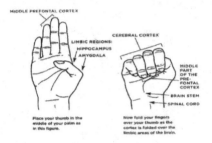

- Make a fist, tucking your thumb inside your other fingers . . .
- Wrist = spinal cord.
- Palm = b r a i n s t e m -regulates body functions, including immune system keeps us breathing, reacts automatically to stimuli like light or sound.
- Thumb = limbic system-center of emotions in the brain differentiate pleasure and pain, tell us what we want and what we fear.
- Fingers = cerebral cortex-"thinking brain"
- Fingertips = prefrontal cortex (PFC)-the area thought to be very important to identity, self-concept, and self-esteem; also an area that can modulate what happens in the limbic system.

You tube link to a video explaining this

Tips to be mindful of when experiencing interpersonal conflict

1. This is a sensitive time. Your spouse, your children, and you will be in fight or flight at times and flip your lids.
2. Pay attention to body sensations that warn you that you are entering fight or flight.
3. Once someone has flipped his or her lid, the person can no longer actively listen and rationalize. It is better for the person to take a mindful minute and come back when he or she has calmed down.

DEAR MAN

The acronym DEAR MAN outlines a strategy for communicating effectively. This strategy will help you express your wants and needs in a way that is respectful to yourself and others. Using DEAR MAN will increase the likelihood of positive outcomes from your interactions.

Describe: Clearly and concisely describe the facts of the situation, without any judgment.

Express: Use "I" statements to express your emotions.

Assert: Clearly state what you want or need. Be specific when giving instructions or making requests.

Reinforce: Reward the other person for responding well to you.

Mindfulness: Being mindful of your goal means not being sidetracked or distracted by other issues.

Appear confident: Use body language to show confidence, even if you don't feel it. Stand up straight, make appropriate eye contact, speak clearly, and avoid fidgeting.

Negotiate: Know the limits of what you are willing to accept but be willing to compromise within them.

SPEAKER-LISTENER TECHNIQUE

Rules for the Speaker

1. Speak for yourself. Talk about your thoughts, feelings, and concerns, not your perceptions or interpretations of the listener's point of view or motives.
2. Use "I" statements and talk about your own point of view.
3. Don't try to read the other person's mind.
4. Talk in small chunks, one topic at a time, one feeling at a time. Start slowly. You will have plenty of opportunity to say all you need; you don't have to say it all at once. Keeping what you say manageable is crucial to helping the listener actively listen.

A good rule of thumb is to keep your statements to just a sentence or two, especially when first learning the technique.

Setting a phone or small sand timer would be a good tool for this exercise.

The timer represents a beginning, middle, and end. It keeps people fair and protects you from losing the message in a monologue or talking in circles.

RULES FOR THE LISTENER

"What I am hearing is ____."

To paraphrase the speaker, briefly repeat what you heard the speaker say, using your own words to ensure you understand what was said.

The key is showing your partner that you are listening as you restate what you heard without any interpretations. If the paraphrase is not quite right (which happens often), the speaker should gently clarify the point. If you genuinely need help understanding some phrase or example, you may ask the speaker to explain or repeat, but you may not question any other aspect of the issue.

As a listener, your job is to speak only to understand your partner.

Any words or gestures to express your opinions, including making faces, are prohibited.

Your task is to understand. Good listening does not equal agreement.

When the point is heard, switch and respond using "I feel" statements. In a relationship, you are either both winning or losing. You are on the same side.

Rules for Both

1. Stay on the topic. Many issues can become involved in one conversation.
2. Use "I feel" statements, and don't point fingers.
3. Be respectful.

The goal is to be validated—heard and understood, not agreed with or ridiculed.

People will forget what you said,
people will forget what you did, but
people will never forget how you
made them feel.

Maya Angelou

REFERENCES

"11 Facts about Military Families." Dosomething.org. Accessed June 10, 2024. https://www.dosomething.org/us/facts/11-facts-about-military-families.

Covey, Sean. 2015. *The 7 Habits of Highly Effective Teens: Workbook*. Mango Media Inc.

"Cycle." In *Merriam-Webster*. Last updated May 29, 2024. https://www.merriam-webster.com/dictionary/cycle.

Dellinger-Bavolek, Juliana. 2000. *Nurturing Book for Babies and Children*. Bluffdale, UT: Family Development Resources, Inc.

"Deployment." In *Merriam-Webster*. Last updated May 30, 2024. https://www.merriam-webster.com/dictionary/deployment.

Halloran, Janie. 2018. *Coping Skills for Kids*. Eau Claire, WI: PESI Publishing and Media.

Hochlan, Jennifer L. 2017. "The 7 Emotional Cycles of Deployment." United States Coast Guard-Pacific Area. Posted August 15, 2017. https://www.pacificarea.uscg.mil/Portals/8/Documents/The 7 Emotional Cycles of Deployment.pdf?ver=2017-08-15-160305-400.

hooah4health.com. 2011. "The Emotional Cycle of Deployment: Deployment." Military.com. Accessed June 23, 2021. https://www.military.com/spouse/military-deployment/emotional-cycle-of-deployment-deployment.html.

Lewis, Teresa. 2022. "Dr. Dan Siegel's Hand Model of the Brain." YouTube. September 6, 2022. Educational video, 3:17. https://www. youtube.com/watch?v=LdaUZ_wbD1c.

Linehan, Marsha M. 2015. *DBT Skills Training Handouts and Worksheets*. Vol. 2. New York: The Guilford Press.

Logan, Kathleen Vestal. 1987. "The Emotional Cycle of Deployment." *Proceedings* 113, no. 2 (February 1987): 1008. https://www.usni.org/magazines/proceedings/1987/february/ emotional-cycle-deployment.

Monson, Thomas S. 2012. "Living the Abundant Life." The Church of Jesus Christ of Latter Day Saints. Posted January 2012. https://www.churchofjesuschrist.org/study/liahona/2012/01/ living-the-abundant-life?lang=eng.

"National Security Decision Directive Number 298." Federation of American Scientists Intelligence Resource Program. Accessed June 5, 2024. https://irp.fas.org/offdocs/nsdd298.htm.

Pincus, Simon H., Robert House, Joseph Christenson, and Lawrence E. Adler. "The Emotional Cycle of Deployment: Military Family Perspective." Military.com. Accessed June 3, 2024. https://www. military.com/spouse/military-deployment/emotional-cycle-of- deployment-military-family.html.

"The struggle you're in today is developing the strength you need for tomorrow. Don't give up." Quotespedia. Accessed June 10, 2024. www.quotespedia.org. https://www.quotespedia.org/authors/r/ robert-tew/the-struggle-youre-in-today-is-developing-the-strength- you-need-for-tomorrow-dont-give-up-robert-tew/.

Rathus, Jill H. and Alec L. Miller. 2015. *DBT Skills Manual for Adolescents.* New York: The Guilford Press.

Robbins, Mel. "Mel Robbins Motivational Quotes to Brighten Your Day." Well Quo. Accessed April 4, 2020. https://wellquo.com/mel-robbins-motivational-quotes-to-brighten-your-day/.

Siegel, Daniel J. 2010. *Mindsight: Change Your Brain and Your Life.* Melbourne: Scribe.

Swales, Michaela A. and Heidi L. Heard. 2009. *Dialectical Behavior Therapy.* New York: Routledge.

Sughesti, F. 2022. "The Power of Breathwork." AIM'N. Posted April 24, 2022. https://www.aimn.com/blogs/news/the-power-of-breathwork#:~:text=When%20breathing%2C%20on%20the%20inhale,to%20completely%20shift%20your%20energy.

"Support for Military Personnel and Families." Military OneSource. Accessed February 16, 2024. https://www.militaryonesource.mil/.

Van Dijk, Sheri. 2012. *DBT Made Simple: A Step-by-Step Guide to Dialectical Behavior Therapy.* Oakland, CA: New Harbinger Publications.

Printed in the United States
by Baker & Taylor Publisher Services